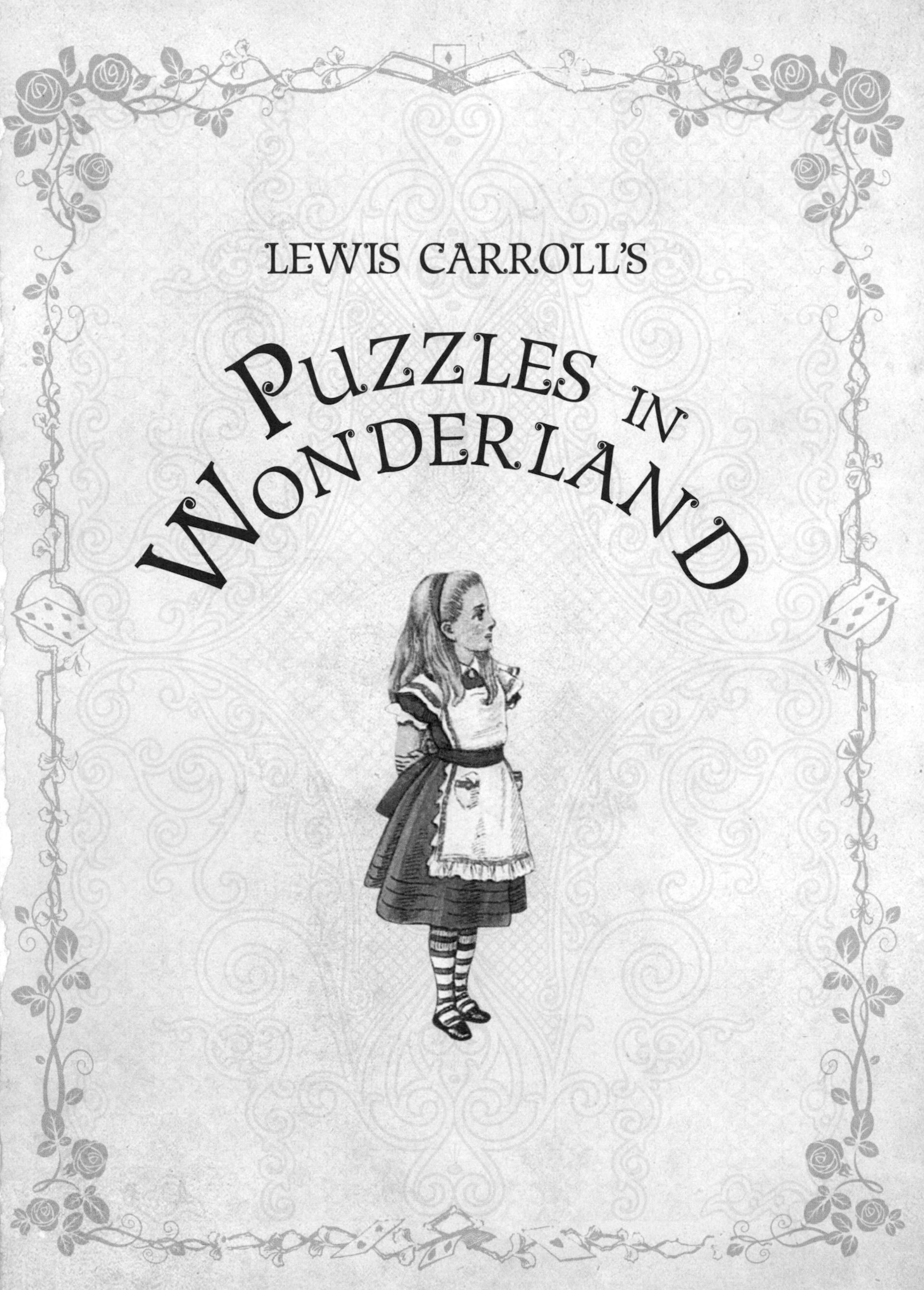

LEWIS CARROLL'S

PUZZLES IN WONDERLAND

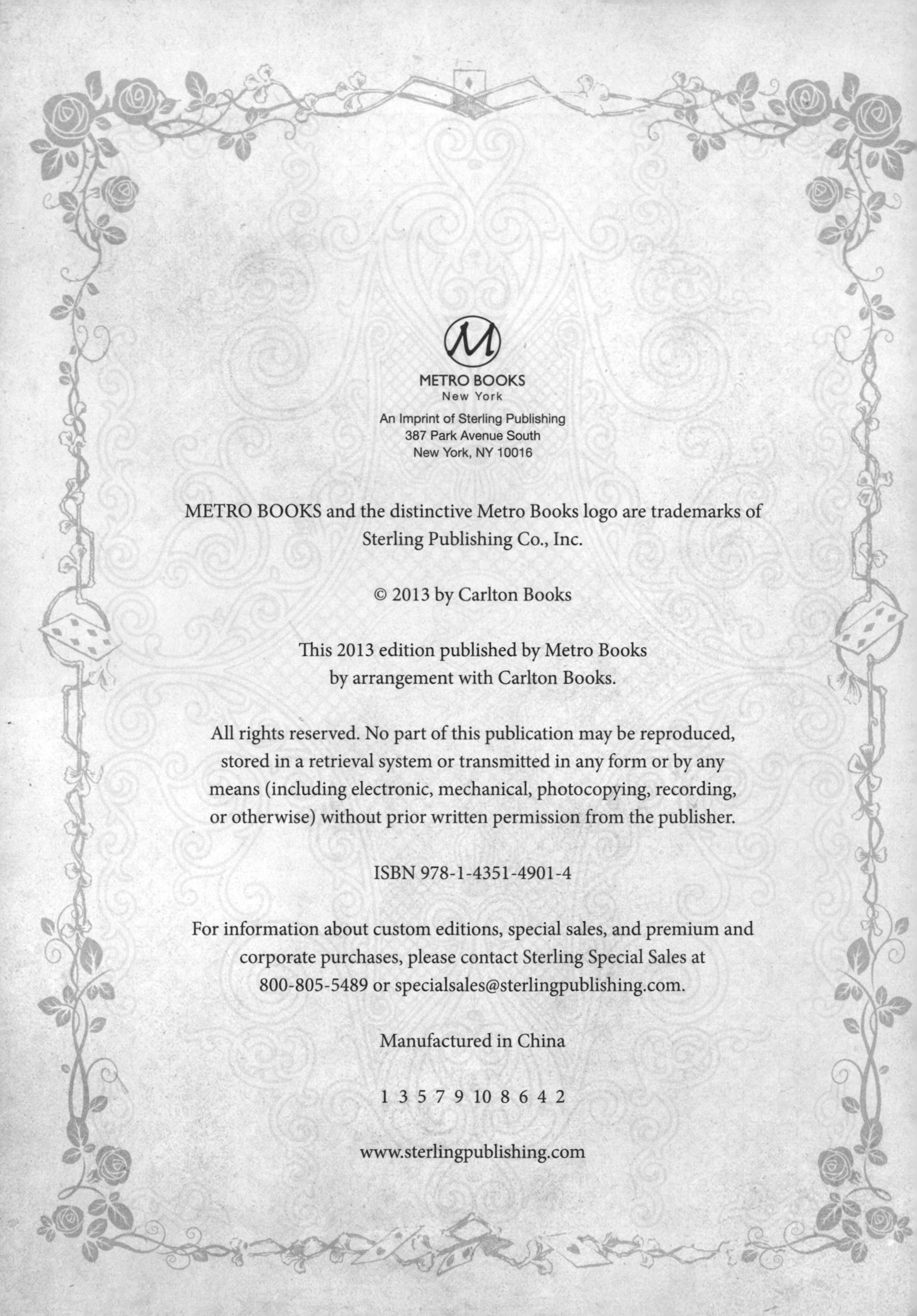

METRO BOOKS
New York

An Imprint of Sterling Publishing
387 Park Avenue South
New York, NY 10016

This 2013 edition published by Metro Books by arrangement with Carlton Books.

ISBN 978-1-4351-4901-4

For information about custom editions, special sales, and premium and corporate purchases, please contact Sterling Special Sales at 800-805-5489 or specialsales@sterlingpublishing.com.

Manufactured in China

1 3 5 7 9 10 8 6 4 2

www.sterlingpublishing.com

LEWIS CARROLL'S

PUZZLES IN WONDERLAND

A frabjous puzzle challenge, inspired by Alice's adventures

R.W. Galland

METRO BOOKS
New York

CONTENTS

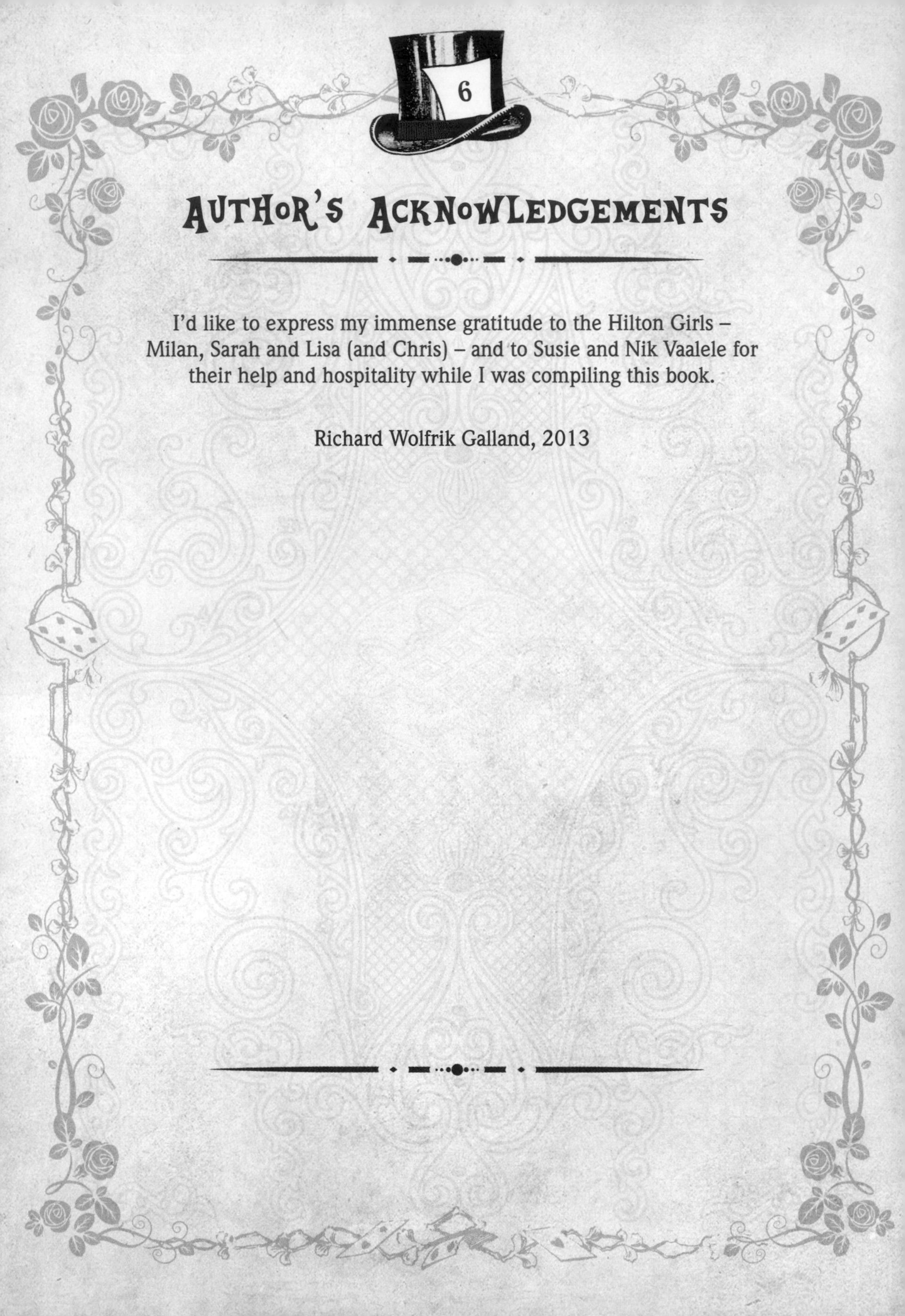

Author's Acknowledgements

I'd like to express my immense gratitude to the Hilton Girls – Milan, Sarah and Lisa (and Chris) – and to Susie and Nik Vaalele for their help and hospitality while I was compiling this book.

Richard Wolfrik Galland, 2013

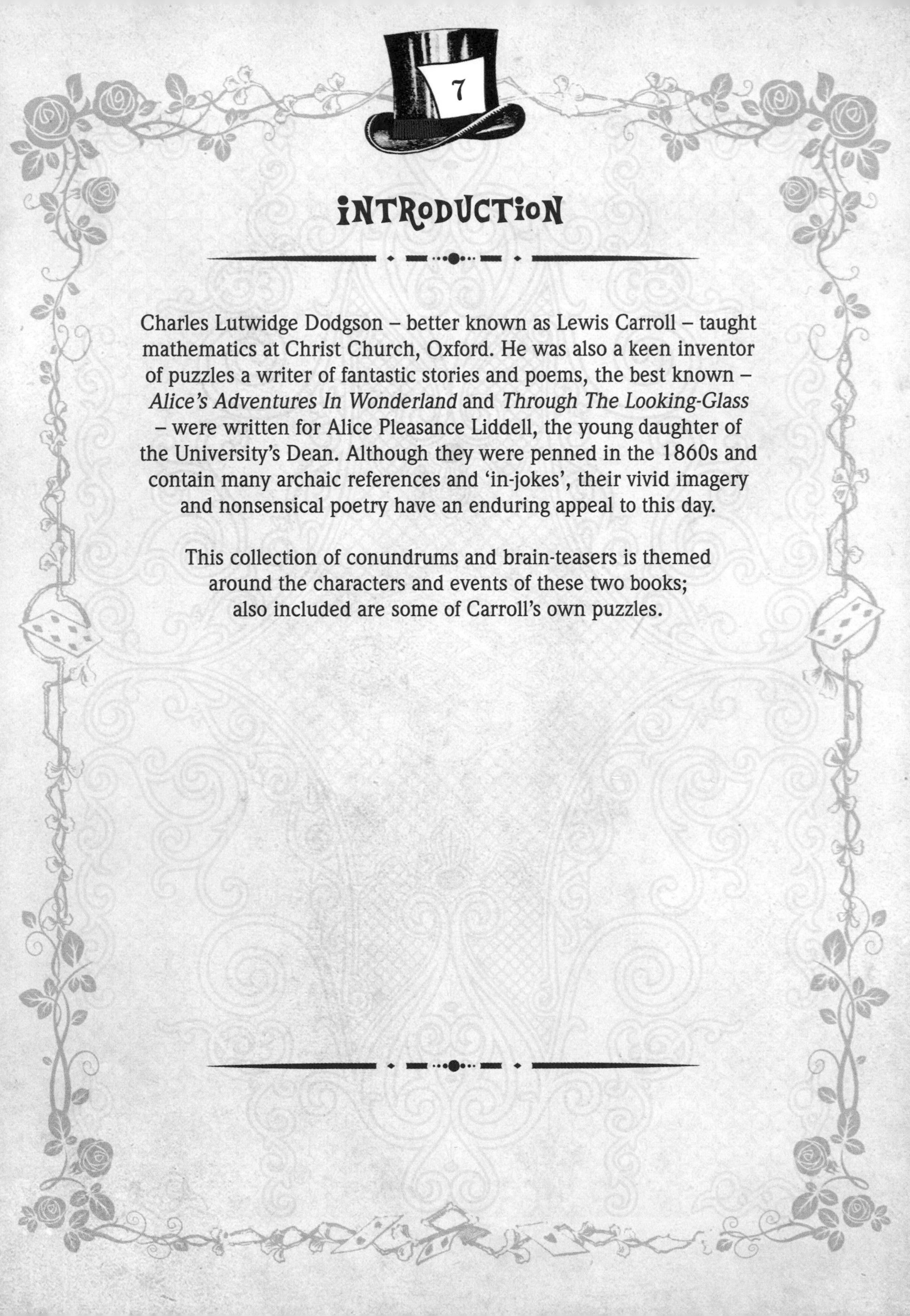

INTRODUCTION

Charles Lutwidge Dodgson – better known as Lewis Carroll – taught mathematics at Christ Church, Oxford. He was also a keen inventor of puzzles a writer of fantastic stories and poems, the best known – *Alice's Adventures In Wonderland* and *Through The Looking-Glass* – were written for Alice Pleasance Liddell, the young daughter of the University's Dean. Although they were penned in the 1860s and contain many archaic references and 'in-jokes', their vivid imagery and nonsensical poetry have an enduring appeal to this day.

This collection of conundrums and brain-teasers is themed around the characters and events of these two books; also included are some of Carroll's own puzzles.

EASY PUZZLES

DRINK ME

TWEEDLE DUM & TWEEDLE DEE

"ARE YOU TWINS?" asked Alice.

"Nohow!" said Dee.

"But we *do* share the same parents," said Dum.

"And we were born on the same day of the same year."

"But we certainly are not twins."

How can this be?

Solution on page 168

Archer

"I ONCE KNEW AN ARCHER,"

recalled the White Knight,

"Who put on a blindfold and knotted it tight.

He had hung up his hat and, though blind as a bat,

When he let loose his arrow, it went straight through the hat!"

"He must have been a very good archer," said Alice.

"Not at all," replied the Knight, "he was the worst archer in the Kingdom."

"A lucky shot, then?" she offered.

"Not at all," replied the Knight, "he could perform the feat a thousand times."

Can you explain?

Solution on page 168

12

A Mock Lamentation

ALICE FOUND THE MOCK TURTLE

sobbing quietly beside a rock pool.

He turned to her and said:

"You take a knife,
And cut me deep,
I am not hurt,
But still you weep."

The Gryphon arrived and joined in mournfully:

"It's said in France,
They love me true,
Chop off my head,
And cry 'boo-hoo'."

"Do you know what we are?" asked the Mock Turtle.

Solution on page 168

Contrariwise!

"I DIDN'T SEE HER ARRIVE because I was standing behind you," said Tweedle Dum.

"Contrariwise!" argued Tweedle Dee "I was standing behind *you*!"

"Nohow!" retorted Dee angrily.

It looked like another fight would ensue.

"Wait!" said Alice, "I think I see what happened."

Can you?

Solution on page 169

SIGNING OFF

ALICE'S JOURNEY across the chess board was starting to befuddle her mind. Then, to her delight, she spied a signpost with four arrows.

"Now I shall be back on my way to becoming a Queen," she said happily. But just as the words had left her mouth, a gust of wind uprooted the sign. Alice picked up the signpost and was surprised to find it still intact. "I have no map and no one to ask for directions," she said to herself, "however am I to find my way now?"

Solution on page 169

SPOT THE DIFFERENCE

There are eight differences between the picture on the left and its mirror image on the right; can you find them?

Solution on page 170

DANGEROUS DECISION

ALICE HAS TO CHOOSE between three doors. The first leads to a maze paved with red-hot coals, the second to a pitch-black room containing a bottomless hole, and the third to the open cage of a lion who hasn't eaten in six months.

Which door should she enter?

Solution on page 171

Rows of Roses

"THERE! THAT'S THE LAST OF THEM!"

declared the first gardener with evident relief.

They had successfully painted the Queen's roses a bright shade of red, with just moments to spare before Her Majesty's arrival.

"Wait!" said the second gardener, his face turning as white as the roses had been, "she said she wanted five rows with four bushes in each row – we've only got two rows of five!"

"She's coming!" shouted the third gardener in terror.

The gardeners only have time to move four of the bushes before the Queen arrives. Is there any way they can make five rows with four bushes in each row?

Solution on page 171

A STICKY QUESTION

A STICK I FOUND that weighed two pound;

I sawed it up one day

In pieces eight of equal weight!

How much did each piece weigh?

Clue: "a quarter of a pound" is not the right answer.

From *Puzzles From Wonderland* by Lewis Carroll

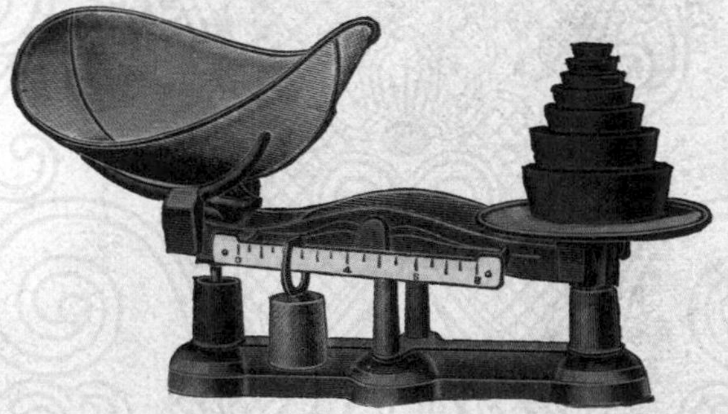

Solution on page 172

TWO RIDDLES

LET ME EAT and I will live,
but give me water
and I will surely die.
What am I?

I WEIGH NOTHING,
but you can see me.
Put me in a bucket of water,
and I'll make it lighter.
What am I?

Solution on page 172

HAT TRICK

THE HATTER, the March Hare, Tweedle Dum, Tweedle Dee, the Carpenter and five other gentlemen – whose names were so dull that they had quite forgotten them – were walking along the beach. Everyone wore hats, which is the proper thing to do when walking along a beach.

Suddenly a gust of wind blew in from the sea, seizing their hats and depositing them on the shingle in a pile.

Each hatless walker reached down to retrieve a hat from the pile. They had sand in their eyes and could not discern one hat from another.

What is the probability that exactly nine of them found their own hat straight away?

Solution on page 173

23

Mirror Image

Only one of the small pictures on the right is a true mirror image of the one on the left. But which one?

A

B

C

D

Solution on page 174

BALL AND CHAIN

"BUT YOU SIMPLY MUST come to the ball," said the Duchess cordially; "everyone will be there."

"I shall," promised Alice.

"Of course you must observe the dress code," said the Duchess as she turned to leave; "every lady must wear a necklace. See you tonight!"

"Oh dear," said Alice, taking the broken necklace from her pocket. There were four pieces of gold chain each made of three links.

She paid a visit to the royal blacksmith.

"Could you make these into a necklace?" she asked him.

The blacksmith replied, "I charge a penny to break a link and a penny to melt it together again. To fit the pieces together, I'll have to break and re-join four links. That will be eight pennies."

"But I only have six pennies" said Alice sadly.

Is there any way Alice can get the necklace fixed?

Solution on page 175

PERFORMANCE

THE HATTER was reciting another of his riddles.

"I always perform under pressure,
In theatres I don't entertain,
Audiences can't stand to see me,
But display me in fury and shame.
What am I?"

Solution on page 175

THE GARDEN OF LIVE FLOWERS

ALICE IS STUCK in the middle of this maze; can you help her to find her way out?

This maze was created by Lewis Carroll for the magazine *Mischmash*.

Solution on page 176

THE WHITE KNIGHT'S JOURNEY

THE WHITE KNIGHT was making his way home. He rode for the first half of the journey, which was fifteen times faster than his normal walking speed. Then he fell off. So for the second half he walked alongside his plodding horse – but he could have walked twice as fast without the hindrance.

Would he have saved time if he had gone all the way on foot without his trusty steed?

If so, how much?

Solution on page 177

TOASTY

"HURRY UP WITH THAT TOAST!"
demanded the Duchess.

The Cook was making French toast in a small pan. After toasting one side of a slice, he turned it over. Each side took 30 seconds.

The pan could only hold two slices. How might he have toasted both sides of three slices in one and a half instead of two minutes?

Solution on page 177

Rose Picking

"BRING ME A ROSE and I'll tell you another story," said the Duchess.

"Oh, not more morals," thought Alice. But she headed off to the gardens nevertheless.

Three gardeners were standing guard beside the rose bushes.

"Taking roses from the garden is a behead-able offence." declared the first gardener.

"But we won't tell the Queen if you pay each of us in turn before you leave," said the second.

"Half of the roses you have, plus two more," added the third.

She left the garden with a single rose as instructed.

But how many did she pick in the first place?

Solution on page 178

SPOT THE DIFFERENCE

There are eight differences between the picture on the left and its mirror image on the right; can you find them?

Solution on page 179

A CAUCUS RACE

"DO HURRY, or you'll never be dry!" called the Dodo.

Alice had to admit that she wasn't really making much of an effort. After all, the race didn't seem to have any rules.

The Dodo can run once around the track in six minutes, while Alice can do it in four minutes. How many minutes will it take for Alice to overtake the Dodo?

Solution on page 180

Poem

THIS POEM APPEARS **at the end of** ***Through The Looking-Glass*****. Something is hidden within its lines.**

Can you say what ... or who?

A boat beneath a sunny sky,
Lingering onward dreamily
In an evening of July –

Children three that nestle near,
Eager eye and willing ear,
Pleased a simple tale to hear –

Long had paled that sunny sky:
Echoes fade and memories die.
Autumn frosts have slain July.

Still she haunts me, phantomwise,
Alice moving under skies
Never seen by waking eyes.

Children yet, the tale to hear,
Eager eye and willing ear,
Lovingly shall nestle near.

In a Wonderland they lie,
Dreaming as the days go by,
Dreaming as the summers die:

Ever drifting down the stream –
Lingering in the golden gleam –
Life, what is it but a dream?

Solution on page 180

THE CHESHIRE'S CLOCK

"WHAT TIME IS IT?" asked Alice.

"Look at the clock," said the Cheshire Cat.

"But I don't see a clock."

"It's invisible."

"Then what use is it?" demanded Alice.

"It chimes every hour on the hour and once each quarter-hour in between."

If Alice hears it chime once, what is the *longest* she must wait to find out what time it is?

Solution on page 181

PEPPER

“HERE! WATCH THE POT FOR ME,” said the Cook. “I need to get some parsnips; I’ll only be half an hour.”

Alice took the ladle from the cook with some trepidation.

“Don’t forget to add pepper in 15 minutes!” said the cook menacingly, “or it’ll be ruined!”

Alice looked around the kitchen but there was no clock to be seen, only two old hourglasses.

One hourglass takes 7 minutes for the sand to run out, and one takes 11 minutes.

What is the best way for Alice to use the hourglasses to time exactly 15 minutes?

Solution on page 181

WHAT'S THE USE?

"HOW SAD IT IS TO BE USEFUL,
when nobody wants you," said the White Knight.

"I'm sure that someone must want you," said Alice sympathetically. As usual she had no idea what he was talking about.

"I didn't mean me," said the Knight, "listen to this –

The one who made me didn't want to use me.

The one who bought me didn't need me.

Anyone who needs me will never know it."

What could the Knight be referring to?

Solution on page 182

FOR THE CHOP

THE QUEEN OF HEARTS had an ultimatum.

She declared to the court, “Let Alice speak her last words. If her statement is true, she will be fed to the Jabberwock. If it is false – off with her head!”

Alice thought for a moment, then she said something that so perplexed the Queen, she was immediately released and granted a royal pardon.

Solution on page 182

MIRROR IMAGE

Solution on page 183

GETTING WARMER

"IT'S RATHER WARM,"

said Alice, who was starting to feel quite drowsy.

"12 degrees," mumbled the White Queen, "it's been getting hotter each day."

"Today's temperature is the product of the last five days," added the Red Queen.

Can you work out what the temperature was each day over the last five days?

Note: all temperatures are whole numbers.

Solution on page 184

Poor Bob

THE CARPENTER was weeping uncontrollably.

"Whatever's the matter?" asked Alice consolingly.

"Bob was found dead in his home this morning!" he cried.

"He was lying beside a tiny puddle of water but he wasn't injured."

"He wasn't very old and he never got sick," added the Walrus.

"The weather was hot and dry – it hadn't rained in weeks!" sobbed the Carpenter.

"Oh, poor Bob," said Alice. "Whatever could have happened to him?"

Can you explain?

Solution on page 184

TARTS

"GIRL! BRING SOME TARTS!"

commanded the Queen.

"Oh, I wish she wouldn't talk as if I were one of her servants," grumbled Alice. But she replied courteously, "How many, Your Majesty?"

The Queen replied:

"*The number of wings on an eagle,*
times the number of hooves on a goat,
times the number of letters in seagull
times the number of ears on a stoat
times the number of zeds in a dozen
times the number of legs on a snake
times the number of leaves on a clover
so tell me... what does that make?"

Solution on page 185

A GAME OF CARDS

TWEEDLE DUM AND TWEEDLE DEE

played cards for a stake of penny a game. At the end, Dum won three games and Dee won three pennies.

How many games did they play?

Solution on page 185

WHO STOLE THE TARTS?

"WHO STOLE MY TARTS?"
demands the Queen of Hearts

The Hatter declares, "'Twas the March Hare!"

The March Hare raves, "The Knave, the Knave!"

The Duchess exclaims, "I cannot be blamed!"

The Knave replies, "The March Hare lies!"

Only one suspect speaks true … but who?

Who stole the tarts?

Solution on page 186

Red Pebble

"OFF WITH HER HEAD!"

The Queen of Hearts has sentenced Alice to be executed again.

So as not to appear unfair, Her Majesty has given Alice one chance to save herself.

The courtyard is covered with tiny black and red pebbles. The Queen pretends to pick one of each colour, and puts them into a bag.

"If she pulls the red pebble from the bag, she shall go free!" declares the Queen.

Alice has noticed the Queen's trick – she has put two *black* pebbles into the bag.

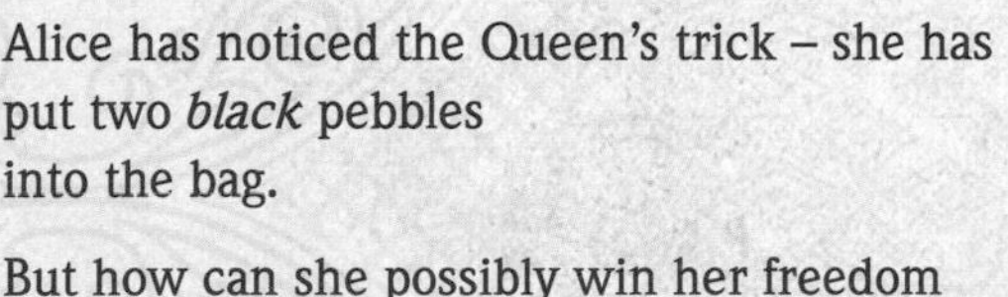

But how can she possibly win her freedom without calling the Queen a cheat?

Solution on page 187

MIRROR IMAGE

Only one of the small silhouettes on the right is a true mirror image of the one on the left. But which one?

A

B

C

D

E

Solution on page 188

ANOTHER MAD TEA-PARTY

THERE ARE THREE GUESTS. Two drink tea, two drink coffee and two drink wine. The one who does not drink wine does not drink coffee, and the one who does not drink coffee does not drink tea.

Which beverage does each guest drink?

Solution on page 189

FLAGS AND BUNTING

THE QUEEN HAS REQUESTED **that two flagpoles, each 100 feet high, be erected with a 150-foot-long rope strung between them. At its lowest point the rope must be 25 feet from the ground.**

How far apart must the flagpoles be?

Solution on page 189

52

CROQUET

"HAVE THE CROQUET PLAYERS ARRIVED?"

asked Alice. "The Queen is rather anxious to know how many are coming."

"They have indeed," intoned the Frog footman.

"All but two of them are Clubs," said the Fish footman.

"All but two of them are Hearts," added the Frog footman.

"And all but two of them are Diamonds," concluded the Fish footman.

"Oh dear, "said Alice, "exactly how many is that?"

Solution on page 190

TIT FOR TAT

THE RED KNIGHT captured three white pawns before he was taken by a rook who was in turn captured by the Red Queen. Her Majesty went on to capture another pawn and a bishop before being captured by the White Queen.

Which side could claim to have gained the most from the battle?

Use the standard values of pieces as follows: pawns are worth 1 point each, knights and bishops are worth 3 points each, rooks are 5 points each and a queen is worth 9 points.

Solution on page 190

Not my cup of tea

"HOW'S THE TEA?' asked the Hatter as Alice stirred her cup.

She was about to take a sip when she noticed –

"There's a fly in it!"

"My humblest apologies," said the fly, "I know when I'm not wanted."

"Let me get you a new cup," offered the March Hare.

Alice took a sip and screwed up her nose.

"But this is the same cup!" she complained.

"How on earth did you know that?" asked the Hatter.

How indeed?

Solution on page 190

MIRROR IMAGE

Only one of the small pictures on the right is a true mirror image of the one on the left. But which one?

A

B

C

D

E

Solution on page 191

WHO'S WHO?

"WHO ARE YOU?" asked Alice

"I'm Tweedle Dum," said the boy on the left.

"I'm Tweedle Dee," said the boy on the right.

"At least one of them is lying," said the Cheshire cat from the tree.

So which is which?

Solution on page 192

THINK OF A NUMBER

From THE HUNTING OF THE SNARK
by Lewis Carroll

Taking Three as the subject to reason about,
A convenient number to state,
We add Seven and Ten, then multiply out
By One Thousand diminished by Eight.

The result we
proceed to divide,
as you see,
By Nine Hundred
and Ninety and
Two:

Then subtract
Seventeen, and the
answer must be
Exactly and
perfectly true.

Solution on page 193

CURIOUS PUZZLES

CLOCK WATCHING

THE WHITE RABBIT'S POCKET WATCH

was in for repairs. He had an accurate clock at home but he'd often forget to wind it so it didn't always show the correct time.

He did, however, remember to wind it up up before heading to the Hatter's.

"Is your clock correct?" he asked the Hatter on arrival.

"Yes, perfectly." was the reply.

After an enjoyable evening of tea and riddles the Rabbit came home and was able to set his own clock correctly. How could he do this without knowing beforehand the length of his journey?

Solution on page 196

Letters

"WHAT ARE YOU DOING?" asked Alice.

"Filing my letters", replied the Hatter. "Care to help?"

The Hatter was busily putting letters of the alphabet into four different drawers in his writing desk. He had already filed:

Drawer 1	A M
Drawer 2	B C D E K
Drawer 3	H I
Drawer 4	F G J L

"Please make sure you put the letters into the correct drawers," said the Hatter, handing her a small looking-glass, before rushing off without another word.

There were thirteen letters still to organize.

T U V W Y N P Q R S Z O X

How should Alice file them?

Solution on page 196

SUITS YOU

THE KNAVE OF CLUBS, the Knave of Spades and the Knave of Diamonds were about to present gifts to the Queen of Hearts.

Each knave carried one gift – a club, a spade and a diamond.

The Knave of Clubs turned to the knave on his right and said, "'Pon my word! Not one of us is holding a gift that matches our suit!"

"I do declare you're right!" replied the knave who was carrying a diamond.

Who was carrying what?

Solution on page 197

TRANSFORMATION

"THERE'S SOMETHING VERY ODD about this looking-glass," said Alice." Things change size and colour and from one thing into another.

"Who knows what this rabbit shall become?"

Solution on page 197

SPOT THE DIFFERENCE

There are ten differences between the picture on the left and its mirror image on the right; can you find them?

Solution on page 198

Heads and Hats

"OFF WITH THEIR HEADS!"

This time it was Alice, the Hatter and the March Hare who had earned the Queen's displeasure.

"Oh but your majesty can't mean to deprive us of our heads?" pleaded Alice. "However will the Hatter try out his hats?"

The Queen produced five hats – three red and two black.

"Close your eyes!" she commanded.

Alice and her companions closed them tightly.

"Put a hat on each of their heads," the Queen ordered her servants, "and throw out the other two.

"Now," said the Queen, "Everyone – with the exception of Alice – open your eyes and tell me what colour hat you are wearing."

"But I can't see!" complained Alice.

"Silence!" shouted the Queen. "If you guess wrong, your head will be forfeit. If none of you guesses correctly, all of your heads will be chopped off this instant."

The Hatter looked at the other two, and said, "I don't know."

The March Hare glanced at the Hatter and Alice and gulped, "I don't know the colour of my hat, either."

Alice sat perfectly still with her eyes closed and smiled.

"Well?" demanded the Queen.

Why was Alice smiling?

Solution on page 199

LYING DAYS

ALICE HAD LOST ALL SENSE OF TIME

and wanted to know what day of the week it was.

She stopped and asked the Lion and the Unicorn. It was well known that the Lion lied all of the time on Monday, Tuesday, and Wednesday. The Unicorn always lied on Thursday, Friday and Saturday.

Alice asked the Lion what day it was and he replied, "Yesterday was one of my lying days."

She couldn't work it out just from the Lion's answer so she asked the Unicorn who replied, "Yesterday was also one of my lying days."

What day was it?

Solution on page 199

Leaves

THE CHESHIRE CAT GRINNED
down from the bough at Alice.

"There are more trees in this wood than there are leaves on any one tree," he purred.

"How do you know?" asked Alice.

"Please don't ask silly questions," said the cat. "So…" he continued, "there must be at least two trees in this wood with the same number of leaves."

Alice frowned, "Is that right?"

"That's a better question," said the Cat, fading once more into a disembodied grin.

"But what's the answer?"

Solution on page 200

THE KING'S CARRIAGE

THE KING LIKES TO PLAY RUMMY at his club on a Wednesday. He is collected by his carriage at five o'clock sharp and taken directly back to the palace.

However, on this particular Wednesday the King finished an hour early and, since it was a sunny afternoon, decided to walk back to the palace.

The royal carriage collected the King along the route, finding His Majesty rather worn out, but he arrived at the palace twenty minutes earlier than usual. How long did the King have to walk before he met the carriage?

Solution on page 200

PAINTED CUBES

IMAGINE that you have some wooden cubes.

You also have six paint tins each containing a different colour of paint.

You paint a cube using a different colour for each of the six faces.

How many different cubes can be painted using the same set of six colours?

Remember that two cubes are different only when it is not possible, by turning one, to make it correspond with the other.

From an original puzzle by Lewis Carroll.

Solution on page 201

A THORNY PROBLEM

"THIS WILL NEVER DO!" shouted the Queen. "These bushes should be in rows – why do you think they are called *rose* bushes?"

As one, the gardeners put their hands to their necks in anticipation of the Queen's punishment.

"I want them replanted in *eight* rows with *three* bushes in each!" demanded the Queen, "otherwise…"

The gardeners quailed. There were only nine rose bushes in total.

Can they comply with Queen's command or will they lose their heads?

Solution on page 201

Spot the Difference

The image on the right is almost a perfect reflection of the image on the left, but there are ten differences; can you spot them?

Solution on page 202

ANOTHER THORNY PROBLEM

THE GARDENERS were more than relieved to have found a solution to the problem of planting the Queen's nine rose bushes in eight rows but their relief was sadly short-lived.

When the Queen returned she was furious.

"Why are there only eight rows?" she bellowed. "There are nine bushes and so there ought to be *nine* rows. Replant them properly or I shall have your heads!"

Oh dear. Can you help the gardeners again?

Solution on page 203

A THIRD THORNY PROBLEM

THE QUEEN stormed back into the garden, just as the gardeners were finishing replanting the nine rose bushes in nine rows.

"It has come to my attention," screeched the Queen, "that the Queen of Spades has arranged her nine gooseberry bushes into nine rows."

A gardener stepped forward, "Now Your Majesty can say the same of her rose bushes," he said proudly.

"I do not wish to say the same!" bellowed the Queen. "How dare you suggest that I would wish to be as mediocre as the Queen of Spades!"

The gardeners cowered beneath her royal displeasure.

"Plant them again!" bellowed the Queen, "and this time in *ten* rows!"

Can it be done?

Solution on page 203

A Head Start

ALICE AND THE DODO ran a race of 100 yards and Alice won by 5 yards.

"It doesn't seem fair," said the Dodo.

"What if I gave you a head start next time?" suggested Alice

Alice started the next race five yards behind the starting line. Both Alice and the Dodo ran the second race at exactly the same speed as before.

What was the result?

Solution on page 204

Hide & Seek

ALICE FOUND the Knave of Hearts and the Knave of Spades in the garden talking to four gardeners.

"We're playing hide and seek," said the Knave of Hearts to Alice.

"We'll lie down and you must pick two," said the Knave of Spades. "If you pick either of us, you win."

"If you lose, we'll tell the Queen where you are," said the Knave of Hearts slyly.

The two knaves and four gardeners threw themselves on the ground so suddenly that Alice couldn't remember who was where. Of course their backs were exactly the same so there was no way of knowing gardener from knave.

"I'll have to choose completely at random," thought Alice glumly.

Which is more likely – that one of the cards Alice chooses will be a knave or that both will be gardeners?

Solution on page 205

EYES OF THE WISE

WHEN THE KING found that his money was nearly all gone, and that he really must live more economically, he decided on sending away most of his Wise Men.

There were some hundreds of them – very fine old men, and magnificently dressed in green velvet gowns with gold buttons; if they had a fault, it was that they always contradicted one another when he asked for their advice – and they certainly ate and drank enormously. So, on the whole, he was rather glad to get rid of them. But there was an old law, which he did not dare to disobey, which said that there must always be:

Seven blind of both eyes

Ten blind of one eye

Five that see with both eyes

Nine that see with one eye

If this be the case, how many wise men could he keep without disobeying the old law?

From the magazine *Puzzles From Wonderland* by Lewis Carroll.

Solution on page 205

SPOT THE DIFFERENCE

The image on the right is almost a perfect reflection of the one on the left, but there are ten differences; can you spot them?

Solution on page 206

STAMPS

THIS MAGIC SQUARE PUZZLE

was invented by Lewis Carroll.

Take nine postal stamps with the following values.

½ d 1d 1½d 2d 2½d 3d 3½d 4d 5d

Put the stamps in the squares of the grid below so that every row, column and diagonal come to the same amount.

You must use all nine stamps and one extra stamp chosen from the denominations listed; this extra stamp may be placed on any square to increase its value by the relevant amount.

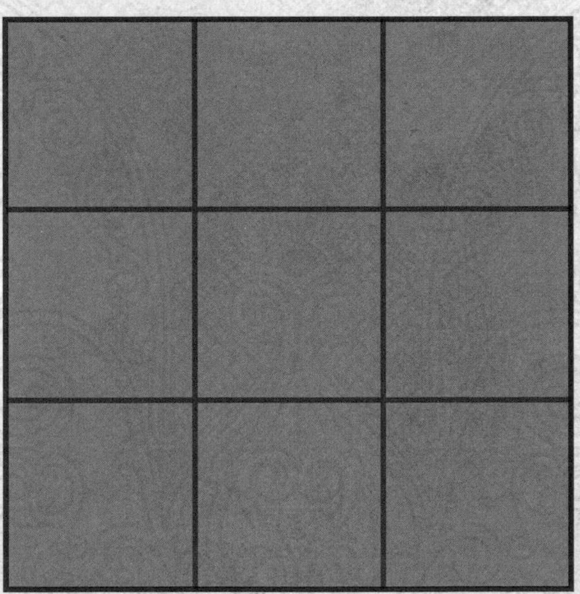

Solution on page 207

THREE CARDS

THREE PLAYING CARDS lay face-down on the path.

"You can go no further until you guess who we are!" came a muffled voice from the ground.

"I really haven't a clue." said Alice.

"We'll give you three." said the voice

"There is a two to the right of a king.

"A diamond will be found to the left of a spade."

"An ace is to the left of a heart. A heart is to the left of a spade."

What did Alice conclude?

Solution on page 207

WATCHMAKER

THE WHITE RABBIT had sent his pocket watch for repairs; unfortunately the watchmaker was one of the Hatter's friends and a little bit...mad.

He did a good job fixing the mechanism but when he attached the hands he mixed up the hour hand and the minute hand. He then set the watch by his own clock. It was six o'clock, so he set the big hand at 12 and the little hand at 6.

The White Rabbit collected his watch gratefully, but some time later he returned to the Watchmaker's shop in a panic.

"Something is wrong! My watch shows the wrong time."

The Watchmaker looked at the watch – it was not much after eight. He pointed to his own clock on the wall and said to the rabbit: "Nonsense; your watch is correct to the second."

The Rabbit was astonished to find that this was correct. He apologised and left.

Early next morning the Rabbit was back in the shop, quite beside himself with displeasure.

"My watch shows the wrong time!"

Again the Watchmaker looked at the watch, which showed a little after seven, and checked it against his wall clock which showed exactly the same time.

"My dear Rabbit, you are quite mistaken. Perhaps you're going … you know … mad?"

Do you know what was going on?

Solution on page 208

SQUARE WINDOW

THE CARPENTER paid a visit to the Walrus, who seemed to be in a miserable state.

"It's my window, "explained the Walrus; "it lets in too much light."

"That's not a problem, " said the Carpenter. "I could put up curtains or blinds if you'd like."

"Oh no," said the Walrus, "I'd like to keep my window as it is: three feet high and three feet wide, perfectly square and unobstructed by shutter or drape."

"Well, that's a tall order, to be certain," said the Carpenter.

However, after some thought, he fetched his tools and was able to adjust the window to the Walrus's satisfaction.

How did he do it?

From a puzzle by Lewis Carroll.

Solution on page 208

MIRROR IMAGE

Only one of the small pictures on the right is a true mirror image of the one on the left. But which one?

A

B

C

D

Solution on page 209

CAKES ON A TRAIN

ON HER LONG TRAIN JOURNEY **Alice became very hungry. Luckily two of her fellow-passengers had cake. One had three small cakes and the other had five.**

They agreed to divide the cakes equally among the three of them.

Alice was extremely grateful and gave the two passengers eight pennies.

How did the passengers divide the money?

Solution on page 209

WORTH THE WEIGHT

THE SHEEP has only three weights for her shop's scales, but with them she can weigh any whole number of pounds from 1 pound to 13 pounds inclusive.

What weights does she have?

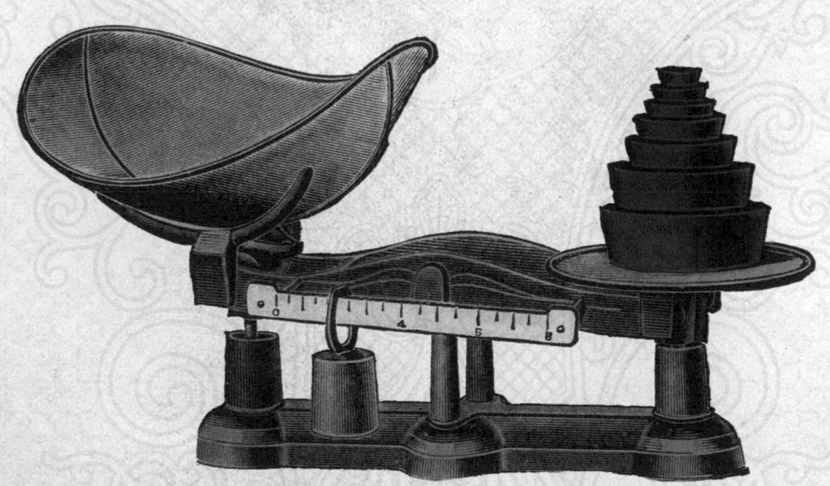

Solution on page 210

YOU ARE OLD, FATHER WILLIAM

"THE DAY BEFORE YESTERDAY I WAS 67,"
said Father William.

"And next year I will be 70!"

How is this possible?

"You are old," said the youth, "one would hardly suppose
That your eye was as steady as ever;
Yet you balance an eel on the end of your nose –
What made you so awfully clever?"

Solution on page 211

Fox, Goose and Corn

THIS CLASSIC PUZZLE

was a favourite of Lewis Carroll.

A man was coming back from the market with a fox, a goose and a sack of corn. He came to a river and had to use a boat that was so tiny he could only take one thing across at a time.

He couldn't leave the fox and goose together because the fox would eat the goose.

He couldn't leave the goose and the sack of corn together because the goose would eat the corn.

How could the man get across the river and keep all of his goods intact?

Solution on page 212

THE SLOW HORSES

THE KING WAS GETTING OLD and increasingly eccentric, so he decided it was time to pass his throne on to one of his two sons.

He decreed that a horse race should be held and that the son who owned the slower horse would become the new king. The sons had no idea how to run a race in which the slowest horse would win so they asked Alice for advice.

With just two words, Alice ensured that the race would be both competitive and fair.

What did she say?

Solution on page 212

SPOT THE DIFFERENCE

The image on the right is almost a perfect mirror image of the one on the left, but there are ten differences; can you spot them?

Solution on page 213

Hang the Hats

THE HATTER had just purchased 10 new hat-stands for his 44 hats.

"Could you hang them up for me?" he asked Alice.

"Oh hang your hats!" retorted Alice, who was becoming tired of these random errands.

"Yes please," said the Hatter, "and could you ensure that you put a different number of hats on each stand?"

Before Alice could clarify her position, the Hatter had rushed out.

Can Alice comply with the Hatter's instructions?

Solution on page 214

THREE SQUARES

Devised by Lewis Carroll

Draw the picture of three squares below with the following rules:

You may not lift your pencil from the paper.

You may not go over the same line twice.

You may not intersect any other line.

Solution on page 214

A KNIGHT ON THE TOWN

THE RED KNIGHT normally rides to the tavern and walks back to the castle, taking him an hour and a half.

When he rides both ways it takes 30 minutes.

How long would it take him to make the round trip on foot?

Solution on page 215

HAT PINS

"ANOTHER SMALL FAVOUR?" asked the Hatter.

"Not on your life," said Alice; "can't you afford a servant?"

"It's only a tiny favour," said the Hatter; "*this* tiny," he added, pulling a very tiny pin from his hat.

"Oh allright then," said Alice.

"Excellent! In the next room there are exactly 1,000 pins and ten large pin cushions. Please could you push the pins into the cushions so that no two cushions have the same number of pins?"

And with that, he rushed away.

"This sounds horribly like the task he gave me with the hat-stands," grumbled Alice, and that was impossible!"

Solution on page 215

Lemon drop or Aniseed?

HUMPTY held out a large paper bag.

“There’s only one sweet left I’m afraid, and it’s either a lemon drop or aniseed; I really can’t remember which.”

“No, really; I couldn’t take your last sweet,” said Alice.

“That’s very considerate,” said Humpty. “I have another lemon drop here; let me put it into the bag and that will be fair, won’t it?”

Alice had to agree.

Humpty shook the bag and offered it to Alice again, who reached in and took out a sweet. It turned out to be a lemon drop.

What is the chance that the sweet remaining in the bag is also a lemon drop?

Adapted from *Pillow Problems* by Lewis Carroll.

Solution on page 216

THE DINNER PARTY

THE GOVERNOR OF KGOVJNI wants to give a very small dinner-party, and invites his father's brother-in-law, his brother's father-in-law, his father-in-law's brother, and his brother-in-law's father.

Can you determine the smallest possible number of guests?

From *Eligible Apartments* by Lewis Carroll.

Solution on page 217

FIFTY POUNDS

THE HATTER found a £50 note on the ground.

When he arrived home he found a bill from the butcher for £50, whom he promptly visited and paid. The butcher in turn used the note to buy a pig from the farmer, and the farmer paid off a carpenter who had fixed his barn. The carpenter paid it to the King as tax he owed. The King used it to pay a debt to the Hatter for a headpiece he had recently purchased. The Hatter recognised the note as the one he had found. By that time it had paid off £250-worth of debts. Then he realized that the note was fake!

What was lost in the whole transaction, and by whom?

Solution on page 218

ALL THE KING'S MEN

"I NEED MEN WHO CAN RIDE FAST and shoot straight!" declared the King. "Our friend Humpty Dumpty is in peril and I need a company who can put him back together!"

One hundred soldiers accompanied the King. Of these, ten had no proficiency in either marksmanship or horse-riding, 75 were proficient marksmen and 83 were proficient horse-riders. How many of the soldiers were proficient in both marksmanship and horse-riding?

Solution on page 219

SWEETS

THE SHEEP put four sweets into a bag – one white, one blue and two red. She shook the bag and took out two sweets without showing them to Alice. After peeking at them, the Sheep said:

"At least one of the sweets is red. But what are the chances that the other sweet is also red?

"One in three?" ventured Alice."

"Wrong!" bleated the Sheep, "try again!"

Solution on page 219

GREAT WALL

HUMPTY DUMPTY **is climbing up a wall sixty feet high. Every minute, he climbs up three feet but slips back two.**

How long does it take for Humpty to reach the top?

Solution on page 220

A Royal Predicament

"I'D LIKE TO GO HOME NOW," **sighed Alice.**

She was facing two identical looking-glasses, one of which – she was reliably informed – would take her home; the other would leave her trapped here for ever.

The Queens knew which was which, but were being curiously cagey.

"You may ask us one question and one question only regarding the looking-glasses, " said the Queens in unison, "but one of us will tell you the truth and the other will lie."

What question should Alice ask, given that she doesn't know which Queen will lie?

Solution on page 220

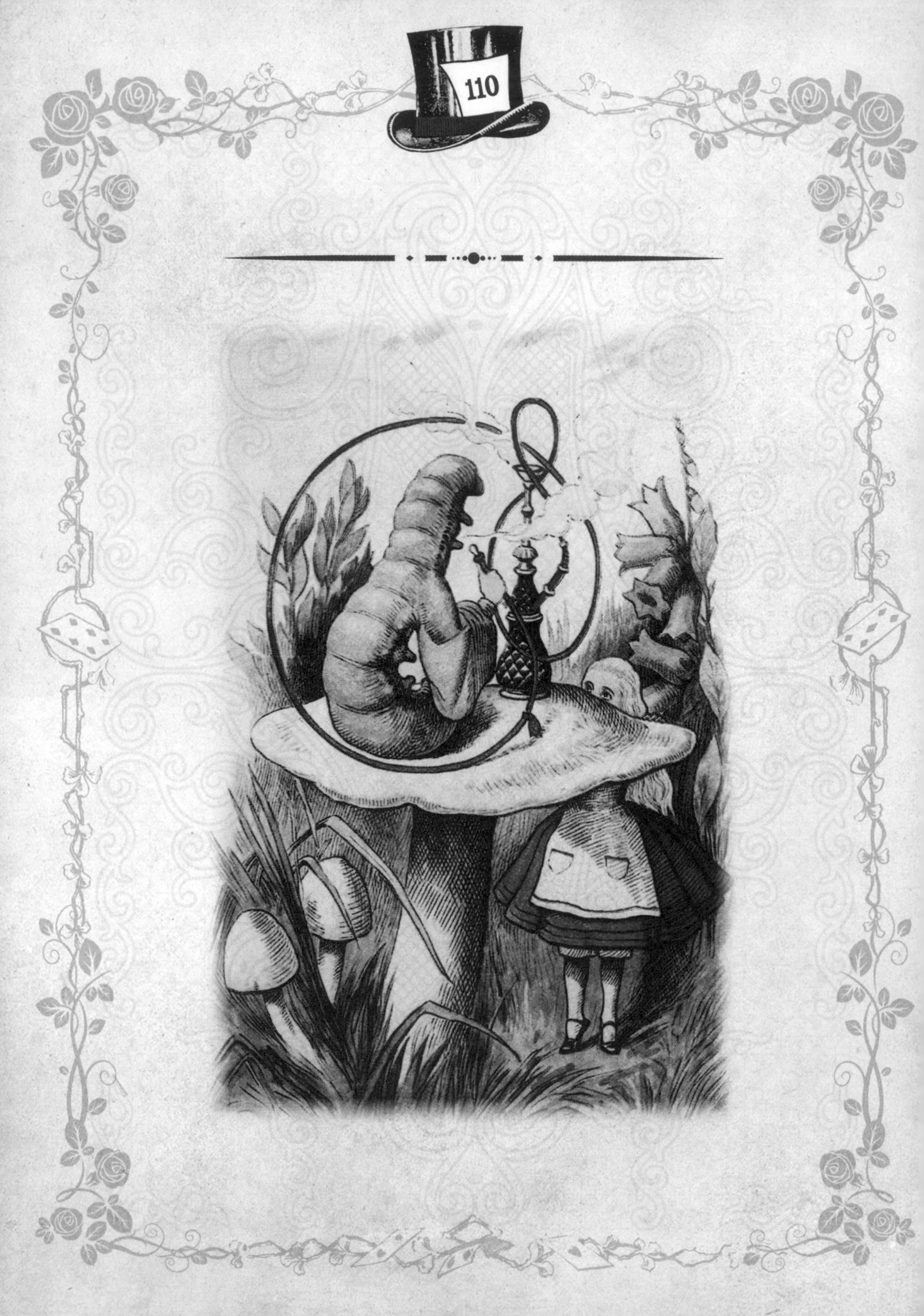

WHO ARE YOU?

"WHO ARE YOU?" said the Caterpillar.

This was not an encouraging opening for a conversation. Alice replied, rather shyly, "I – I hardly know, Sir, just at present – at least I know who I was when I got up this morning, but I think I must have been changed several times since then."

"What do you mean by that?" said the Caterpillar, sternly. "Explain yourself!"

Help Alice to sort herself out by putting the letters of her name into the magic square below. Each column, each row and both long diagonals must contain the name 'ALICE'.

A	L	I	C	E
	E	A	L	
		C		A
	A	L		
		E		

Solution on page 221

HARDER PUZZLES

MULTIPLICATION

"LET ME SEE: **four times five is twelve, and four times six is thirteen, and four times seven is – oh dear! I shall never get to twenty at this rate!"**

Why not?

Solution on page 224

WHAT'S TODAY?

TIME seemed to move differently in Wonderland.

At length Alice asked the Dormouse, "What day is it?"

The Dormouse replied sleepily, "When the day after tomorrow is yesterday, today will be as far from Sunday as today was from Sunday when the day before yesterday was tomorrow."

Was Alice any the wiser?

Solution on page 225

SPOT THE DIFFERENCE

The image on the right is almost a perfect mirror image of the one on the left, but there are eleven differences; can you spot them?

Solution on page 226

JELLY

THE GUESTS were sitting around a circular table so that each guest had two neighbours and each had been served a number of spoonfuls of jelly.

The first had one spoonful more than the second, who had one more than the third, and so on. The first guest gave one spoonful to the second, who gave two spoonfuls to the third, and so on, each giving one more spoonful of jelly than they received for as long as possible.

There were finally two neighbours, one of whom had four times as much jelly as the other.

How many guests were there?

How many spoonfuls had the guest who started with the least number?

Adapted from *Pillow Problems* by Lewis Carroll.

Solution on page 227

THE DUMPTY PICNIC

HUMPTY DUMPTY was safely reinstalled in the King's castle, with a penthouse suite in the highest tower, along with his wife Frumpty and son Numpty.

The well-meaning King, remembering that Humpty and his family had an aversion to stairs, had constructed a rope pulley elevator with baskets on either end. It was designed so that when one basket was on the ground, the other would be at the tower's window.

Humpty weighed 195lbs, Frumpty weighed 105lbs and Numpty 90lbs. The family also had a picnic hamper which weighed 75lbs. Getting into the basket while the other end was empty would be disastrous, but Humpty calculated that if the difference in weight between the two baskets was less than 16lbs, the drop would not turn him or his loved ones into a courtyard omelette.

How did Humpty and his family leave the tower to go on a picnic?

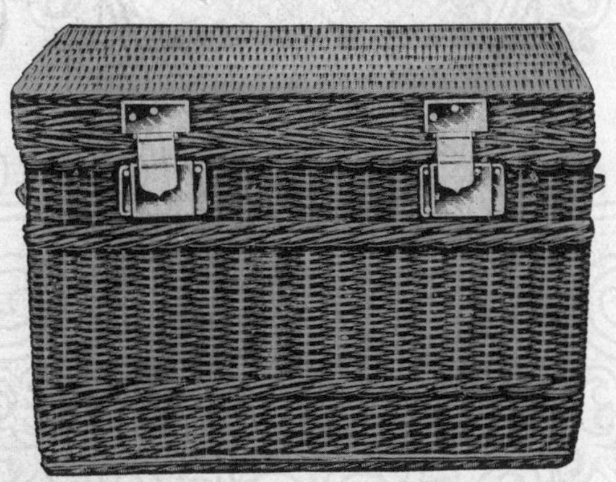

Solution on page 228

DRINK ME?

"PLEASE, YOUR MAJESTY, I need something to return me to my proper size," said Alice.

"Sit down, dear." said the White Queen kindly, "let me see…"

The Queen took two cauldrons, one made of iron, one of bronze. Into the iron cauldron she poured a quart of growth potion and into the bronze a quart of shrinking potion. Alice noticed that her measurements were very precise and she didn't spill a drop.

"I just need to make some adjustments," said the Queen.

She took three ladles of potion from the iron cauldron and poured them into the bronze cauldron and stirred it vigorously.

"Almost there."

She then transferred two ladles from the bronze cauldron back to the iron cauldron and added a pinch of cinnamon to both potions. After stirring them thoroughly she transferred a ladle from the iron cauldron to the bronze cauldron. Finally, she transferred a further two ladles from the bronze cauldron to the iron cauldron.

The Queen surveyed both cauldrons carefully and was satisfied that each contained a quart of potion.

"There!" she declared, "perfect."

"But which one will make me shorter?" asked Alice.

Solution on page 229

CLAM BAKE

FOUR OYSTERS were lying on the beach soaking up the sun; they were Harry, Tom, Peter and Simon.

"I say," said Harry to Simon, "do you realize that Peter is the same relation to Tom as I am to you?"

"Yes," replied Simon, "and you are the same relation to Tom as Peter is to you."

How are the four related?

Solution on page 229

Spot the Difference

The image on the right is almost a perfect mirror image of the one on the left, but there are ten differences; can you spot them?

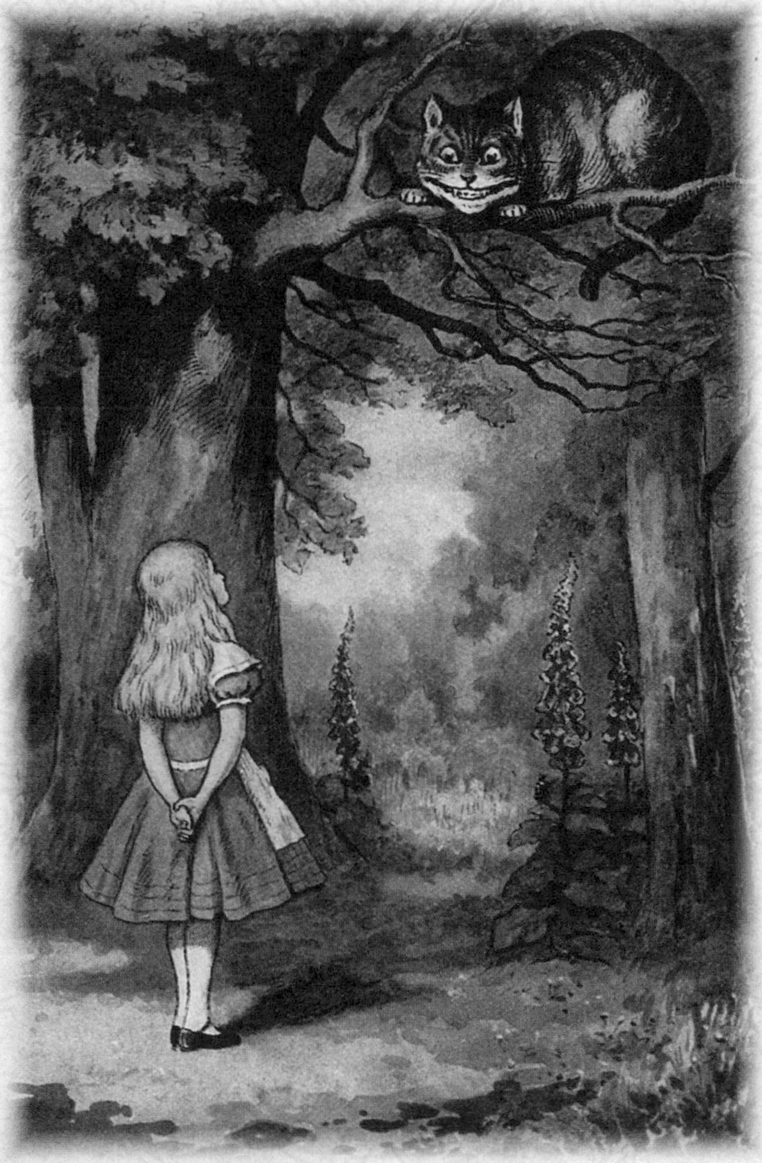

Solution on page 230

Royal Scandal

"WHY IS EVERYONE SO GRUMPY?"
asked Alice.

"It's the Duke's funeral," replied the Footman, "and we've just learned that all this time he had been married to the sister of his own widow!"

"I really ought to have breakfast soon," said Alice, "I'm sure I've exceeded my quota of impossible things to believe."

"Oh, it's quite possible," said the Footman.

How?

Solution on page 231

THE QUEEN'S GARDEN

THE QUEEN OF HEARTS' DETERMINATION

to upstage her rivals in horticultural matters led to the construction of a new garden.

The garden was almost square, just half a yard longer than it was wide, entirely divided by a single spiralling path, a full yard wide, which terminated in the centre of the garden where the royal rose bushes were located.

The path was 7,788 yards in length. What were the dimensions of the garden?

Solution on page 231

THE LION AND THE UNICORN

THE LION AND UNICORN were arguing.

"Age before beauty!" insisted the Lion.

"How old *are* you?" Alice asked them.

"What a curious question," said the Unicorn. "The answer is simple – ."

"The Lion is twice as old as I was when the Lion was half as old as I will be when I'm three times as old as the Lion was when he was three times as old me."

"I see," said Alice with no conviction whatsoever.

"Together we have 44 years," said the Lion.

So, how old is The Unicorn?

Solution on page 232

BLIND DEREK

“DID YOU EVER HEAR the tale of Blind Derek – the cleverest pirate ever to sail the ocean?” asked the Walrus.

“I can’t say I did,” said Alice, although she had a feeling that she was going to.

“Four pirates, Albert, Barney, Colin and Blind Derek, had been captured by King Prawn the Merciless. He decided to set them a challenge so that they might win back their freedom.”

“He wasn’t completely merciless, then,” said Alice.

The Lobster gave her a disapproving scowl. “They were each given a chest: one containing three gold coins, one containing two gold coins and a silver coin, one containing a gold coin and two silver coins, and a fourth containing three silver coins.

“Each chest had a label on it reading ‘Three Gold’ or ‘Two Gold, One Silver’ or ‘One Gold, Two Silver’ or ‘Three Silver’.

“The pirates were told that none of the four labels correctly described the contents of the chest to which it was attached. Each pirate saw only the label of the chest assigned to him. Each one was then asked to close his eyes, remove two coins from his chest, and then try to guess the colour of the remaining coin.

“Albert removed two gold coins, then announced, ‘I’ve drawn two gold coins, and I know the colour of the third coin.’ Barney removed a silver and a gold coin, and stated, ‘I have drawn one silver and one gold coin, and I know the colour of the third coin.’ Colin removed two silver coins, looked at the label, and said ‘I have drawn two silver coins, but I can't tell what the colour of the third coin is.’

“Finally, Blind Derek – who was as sightless as his namesake and could not read the label on his chest – declared: ‘I don't need to remove any coins from my chest. I know the colour of all three. What's more, I know the colour of the third coin in each of the other chests as well.’

“Impossible as it sounds, Derek was correct and secured the release of himself and his ship-mates.”

Can you say how Blind Derek found the answer?

Solution on page 233

SPOT THE DIFFERENCE

The image on the right is almost a perfect mirror image of the one on the left, but there are ten differences; can you spot them?

Solution on page 234

RIVER MADNESS

THE HATTER was enjoying a carefree afternoon in his rowing boat on the river. The river flowed at a speed of 3 miles an hour and the boat drifted down the river at the same rate.

Just as he decided to row upstream, the wind blew his hat from his head and into the water beside the boat. However, he didn't notice that his hat was gone until he had rowed 5 miles upstream, at which point he immediately started rowing back downstream to retrieve his hat.

The Hatter's rowing speed in still water was a constant 5 miles an hour, but when rowing upstream his speed relative to the shore was only 2 miles an hour, subtracting the flow of the river. Rowing downstream, his speed relative to the shore was 8 miles an hour because he was now adding the river speed.

If the Hatter lost his hat at 2 o'clock in the afternoon, what was the time when he retrieved it?

Solution on page 235

Biscuits

"OH DEAR, OH DEAR," bleated the Sheep.
"I've just received three tins of biscuits."

"That sounds like excellent news," said Alice, "but why are you so upset?"

She saw that each tin had a clear hand-written label: 'Ginger snaps', 'Shortbread', and 'Ginger snaps and shortbread'. Her tummy started to rumble.

The Sheep continued, "The baker just told me that none of the tins are labelled correctly."

Alice scrutinized the contents. "All the biscuits look the same," she noted.

"That's because they're covered in chocolate, dear."

"Can we taste them and find out which is which?" asked Alice enthusiastically.

The sheep sighed, "Only if you can find a way by eating just *one* biscuit. I can't afford to lose more than that."

Can Alice label the tins correctly if she is only allowed to taste just one biscuit from just one of the tins?

Solution on page 236

TOING AND FROING

"YOU MAY KEEP YOUR HEAD," said the Queen of Hearts to Alice, "in exchange for a small service."

Alice had become used to performing these tasks in order to avoid summary execution, so she merely nodded.

The Queen continued, "In this wheelbarrow are 100 rose bulbs. I want you to plant them in a row along my new pathway.

"You must take one bulb at a time and plant them one yard apart in a straight line, starting one yard from the wheelbarrow. After each planting you must return to the wheelbarrow and take another bulb unless there are none left, in which case you may stop."

How many yards would Alice have to walk to accomplish the task?

Solution on page 237

NEVER ASK A CATERPILLAR

"OH, NO; my watch has stopped again!" said the White Rabbit to no one in particular.

"That is unfortunate," intoned the Caterpillar from atop his fungal perch.

"Ah... hello; I didn't see you up there. I don't suppose *you* could give me the correct time, could you?" asked the Rabbit. His uncertainty came from his long acquaintance with the Caterpillar, who often gave cryptic answers to straightforward questions.

The Caterpillar did not disappoint –

"Your supposition is incorrect. If you take a quarter of the time elapsed since midday today, and a half of the time remaining between now and midday tomorrow, and add these two values together, you will have the correct time."

So, what time was it?

Solution on page 237

ON HER MAJESTY'S SERVICE

ALICE APPROACHED THE PALACE with trepidation. You could never be sure what sort of mood the Queen would be in. She was greeted coldly by the Fish Footman at the door.

"Hello again," said Alice. "You always seem to be on duty. Don't you ever have a day off?"

The Fish replied: "Her majesty has three footmen: myself, Fox and Ferret. At least one of the footmen has to be on duty at all times. However, there are certain rules which must be observed or heads will roll:

"If I am off-duty, and Fox is off-duty, Ferret must be on duty. If Fox is off-duty, Ferret must also be off-duty."

Could the Fish Footman ever go off-duty?

Solution on page 238

A Wonderful Number

THERE IS A SIX-DIGIT NUMBER that when multiplied by 2, 3, 4, 5 or 6, remains made up of the same digits in the same order. All that changes is the place where the number starts.

Can you find out what it is?

Solution on page 238

THE QUEEN'S TREASURER

THE TREASURER stood before the Queen of Hearts, accused of dishonesty, incompetence and wearing the wrong shoes.

As ever the Queen wished to be seen as firm but fair, so she asked him:

"How much larger is four-fourths than three-fourths?"

"Why, a fourth, Your Majesty." replied the treasurer.

"Off with his head!" commanded the Queen.

What had the treasurer done wrong?

Solution on page 239

A SHORT SPRING

"WE HAD A VERY SHORT SPRINGTIME in Wonderland this year," said the Caterpillar.

"How short?" asked Alice.

"In the springtime, if it rains in the afternoon, it is always clear in the morning, and when it rains in the morning, it is clear in the afternoon. This year it rained on 9 days, and was clear on 6 afternoons and 7 mornings."

So, how long was the spring?

Solution on page 239

SPOT THE DIFFERENCE

The image on the right is almost a perfect mirror image of the one on the left, but there are ten differences; can you spot them?

Solution on page **240**

FATHER WILLIAM'S SONS

FATHER WILLIAM has three sons.
On the 21st birthday of one of the sons, William said:
"The ages of two of you added together is equal to double that of the third."

One of the sons recalled, "At one point, two of our ages added together had been equal to the third."

The son who was celebrating his birthday said "My total age, on that earlier occasion, was one and a half times greater than the number of years that had passed since then."

How old are Father William's sons?

Solution on page 241

INSTANT MESSAGING

THE QUEEN, the Duchess and the Frog Footman start at the same spot on a straight road. The two great ladies are currently not talking to one another so the Footman must pass messages between them.

The Queen walks forward at 4 miles per hour; the Duchess walks forward at 3 miles per hour. Meanwhile, the Frog Footman races back and forth between them at 10 miles per hour. Assuming that each reversal of direction of the Footman is instantaneous, where is he and which way is he facing after one hour?

Solution on page 242

A Nice Day for a Walk

A PAIR OF CARRIAGES regularly travel both ways between the palaces of the Red and White Queens. The journey takes a quarter of an hour, so the traps simultaneously depart in each direction every 15 minutes.

Alice and the Red Queen are walking along the same route from the White Queen's palace and set out at the same time as a carriage does. Twelve and a half minutes later, they meet a carriage coming back the other way. How much longer will it be before they are overtaken by that carriage on its journey back out?

Solution on page 242

THE KING OF DIAMONDS

THE KING of Diamonds left a very complicated will giving instructions on how his collection of precious gemstones was to be distributed to his ten children – five sons and five daughters.

The instructions he gave were that first one gemstone was to be given to his faithful footman, then exactly a fifth of those remaining had to go to his eldest son. Another gem was then given to the footman, then exactly a fifth of those still remaining went to his second eldest son. This procedure was then repeated exactly until all his five sons had received a share, and the footman had been given five gems. Then, after the fifth son had taken his share, the gemstones still remaining were to be equally divided between his five daughters.

How many gemstones did the King have in his collection?

Solution on page 243

SPOT THE DIFFERENCE

The image on the right is almost a perfect mirror image of the one on the left, but there are ten differences; can you spot them?

Solution on page 244

A GAME OF BRIDGE

THE QUEEN OF HEARTS had invited the Queens of Spades, Diamonds and Clubs over to her palace for their weekly game of bridge.

She had dealt half of the cards when she was interrupted by her herald. After hearing the herald's message and sentencing him to death for interrupting her game, she returned to the table.

Unfortunately no-one could remember where she had dealt the last card. Without knowing the number of cards in any of the four partly-dealt hands, or the number of cards yet to be dealt, how could the Queen continue to deal accurately, with everyone getting exactly the same cards she would have had if the deal had not been interrupted?

Solution on page 245

YOU AREN'T OLD, FATHER WILLIAM

"HOW OLD are you really, Father William?" asked Alice. "You seem much younger than I imagined."

"In six years' time," replied William, "I'll be one and a quarter times as old as I was four years ago."

How old is Father William?

Solution on page 245

THREE IS A CROWD

"I CHALLENGE YOU TO A TRUEL!"

shouted the Red Knight.

"And I accept!" retorted the White Knight.

The two knights turned to Alice. "We challenge you to a truel!"

"But why?" she asked. "Your fight has nothing to do with me!"

"It's very rude to exclude people," said the Red Knight. "Now, arm yourself!"

Each was provided with a slingshot and an unlimited supply of ammunition, which turned out to be potatoes.

"We must decide on a firing order," said the White Knight. "Let's practise on some targets and let the worst shoot first."

The White Knight proved to be an excellent marksman and didn't miss a single target. The Red Knight was successful two out of three times on average and Alice, after some practice, found that she was accurate about a third of the time.

Alice has the first shot. At whom should she shoot?

Solution on page 246

151

To Catch a Dodo

"CATCH ME IF YOU CAN!" shouted the Dodo.

The Caucus Race was experiencing another sudden and altogether pointless change of rules. However, Alice had long become accustomed to such irregularities and immediately set off in pursuit of the demented bird.

She was standing 250 yards due south of the Dodo. Both began running at the same time and ran with uniform speeds. The Dodo ran due east. Instead of running north-east on a straight line, Alice ran so that at every instant she was running directly towards the Dodo.

Assuming that Alice ran one and one-third times faster than the Dodo, how far did the Dodo run before he was caught?

Solution on page 247

KINGS AND QUEENS

THREE CARDS have been removed from an ordinary pack and placed face-down in a row.

To the right of a King there are one or two Queens. To the left of a Queen there are one or two Queens. To the left of a Heart there are one or two Spades. To the right of a Spade there are one or two Spades.

What are the three cards?

Solution on page 248

QUEENS' MOVE

"TO BE WORTHY of becoming a queen you must prove your skill at chess, my dear," said the White Queen.

Alice had won and lost against both queens, and had noticed that the White Queen was a better player than the Red Queen.

"I think you're almost ready," said the Red Queen. "All that remains is for you to win two games out of three in a row with alternate opponents."

Which Queen should Alice play first to maximise her chances of winning two games in a row?

Solution on page 249

A FAIR DEAL?

ALICE SHUFFLED a deck of cards, then dealt them face-up, one at a time.

As she dealt she recited aloud the names of all the cards in the deck in a predetermined order:

"Ace of spades, two of spades, three of spades..."

And so on to the King of Spades: then the same for hearts, diamonds and clubs.

Is there an even chance that at least one card she turns up will be the same as the card she names out loud?

Solution on page 249

THE NORTH POLE

"IS IT ME, or has it become rather chilly?" asked Alice, kicking snow from the toe of her shoe.

"I believe we're heading towards the North Pole," said the White Rabbit, consulting his pocket watch which had, curiously, become a compass.

The two trudged on and eventually reached the Pole. Having passed over it, the Rabbit turned about to look North.

"East should now be on the left-hand side and West on the right-hand side," said the Rabbit, "but the compass points are still the same!"

What is the explanation?

Solution on page 250

SWEET SISTERS

THREE SISTERS agreed to share out a bag of sweets in proportion to their ages. The sum of their ages was 17½ years, and the bag contained 770 sweets. For every sweet Alice took, Edith took three, and for every six that Alice took, Lorena took seven.

How many sweets did each girl take, and what are their respective ages?

Solution on page 250

THE QUEEN'S MARBLES

ALICE ENTERED the Queen of Heart's courtyard to see an all-too-familiar sight: a prisoner facing the executioner's axe and being offered his liberty if he could solve a headache-inducing conundrum. This time it was the White Rabbit's turn to face summary decapitation.

"What is it this time?" asked Alice crossly.

The Queen was outraged at the impertinence: "Off with her…"

"I'm a Queen myself now," interrupted Alice, "so you can't have my head. Just tell me the puzzle so I can rescue my dear friend."

"The prisoner stands accused of misplacing Her Majesty's marbles," announced the Frog Footman. "The puzzlement must fit the crime!"

The Footman presented two bags. "These bags each contain three red, three white, and three black marbles.

"Without looking, the prisoner must take the largest number of marbles that it is possible to remove from the first bag while still being sure that at least one of each colour remains. These marbles are put into the second bag. Then he transfers back – without looking – the smallest possible number of marbles that will ensure that there are at least two of each colour in the first bag.

"To secure his release the prisoner must say how many marbles remain in the second bag."

"I see," said Alice with a sigh.

What answer did she give?

Solution on page 251

OYSTERS FOR SALE

THE WALRUS and the Carpenter had caught a haul of oysters.

They sold all of them, receiving for each oyster the same number of pounds as there were oysters in the haul. The money was given to them in £10 notes except for an excess amount, which was in £1 coins. They divided the notes between them by placing them on a table and alternately taking a note until there were none left. The Walrus complained that this was not fair because the Carpenter took both the first and last notes and thus got £10 more. To even things up somewhat, the Carpenter gave the Walrus all the pound coins, but The Walrus argued that he was still owed some money. The Carpenter agreed to give The Walrus a cheque to make the total amounts equal. What was the value of the cheque?

Solution on page 252

SPOT THE DIFFERENCE

The image on the right is almost a perfect mirror image of the one on the left, but there are ten differences; can you spot them?

Solution on page 253

A Mad Bicycle Ride

THE HATTER rode his bicycle one mile in three minutes with the wind, and returned in four minutes against the wind.

Assuming that he always applies the same force to his pedals, how long would it take him to ride a mile if there were no wind?

Solution on page 254

Another Looking-Glass

"ANOTHER LOOKING-GLASS," said Alice. "Do you think this one will take me home?"

"Without a doubt," said the Rabbit, "but look; there's a puzzle to be solved first."

A sign above the looking-glass read:

Twenty were called, but nineteen came,

Move just one pair,

Make both the same.

On either side of the looking-glass was a column of removable round wooden pegs each inscribed with a number, like so:

3	**1**
4	**2**
5	**7**
8	**9**

"At least it's just simple addition this time," said Alice "the left-hand column adds up to 20 and the right makes 19."

"But which pair of numbers can you move to make both columns the same?" asked the Rabbit.

Solution on page 254

AFTERMATH

THE FURIOUS BATTLE had raged for most of the day and now both sides were taking a breather.

"Herald! What's the damage?" demanded the King.

"Out of 100 men," said the herald, "64 have lost their swords, 62 have lost their shields, 92 have lost their courage, and 87 have lost their minds."

"That's no excuse for laziness," said the King; "only those who have lost their swords, their shields, their courage *and* their minds will be exempt from the next battle!"

What is the minimum number of soldiers who will not have to fight?

Solution on page 255

EASY SOLUTIONS

Tweedle Dum & Tweedle Dee

They might be part of a set of triplets, quads, quins… or more!

Archer

The archer hung his hat *on the arrow* before firing it.

A Mock Lamentation

Alice replied, "Why, you're both onions!"

CONTRARIWISE!

They were standing back to back.

SIGNING OFF

If Alice replaces the sign with the name of the place she has just visited pointing in the right direction, all the other arms will be pointing in the right direction too.

SPOT THE DIFFERENCE

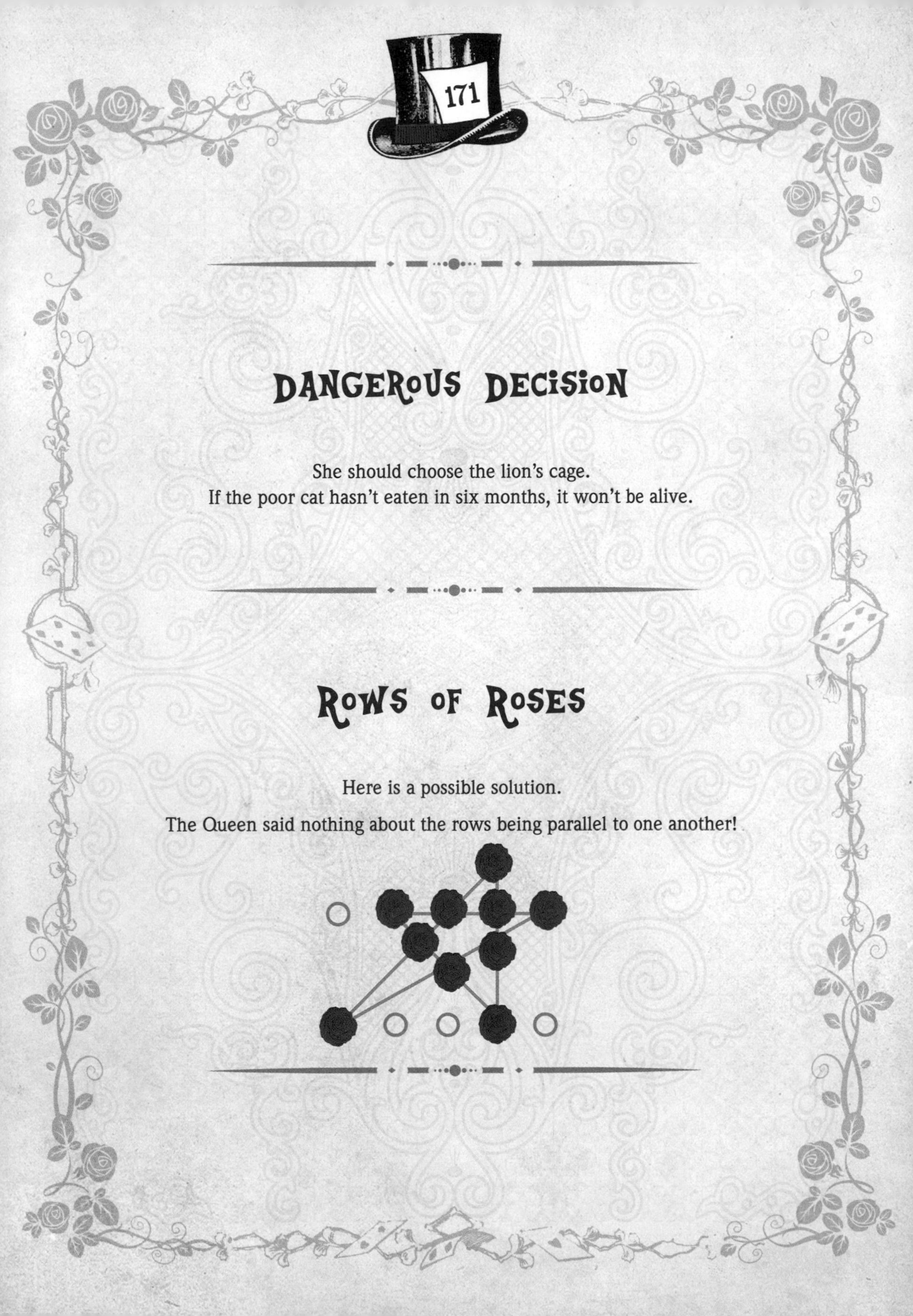

DANGEROUS DECISION

She should choose the lion's cage.
If the poor cat hasn't eaten in six months, it won't be alive.

ROWS OF ROSES

Here is a possible solution.

The Queen said nothing about the rows being parallel to one another!

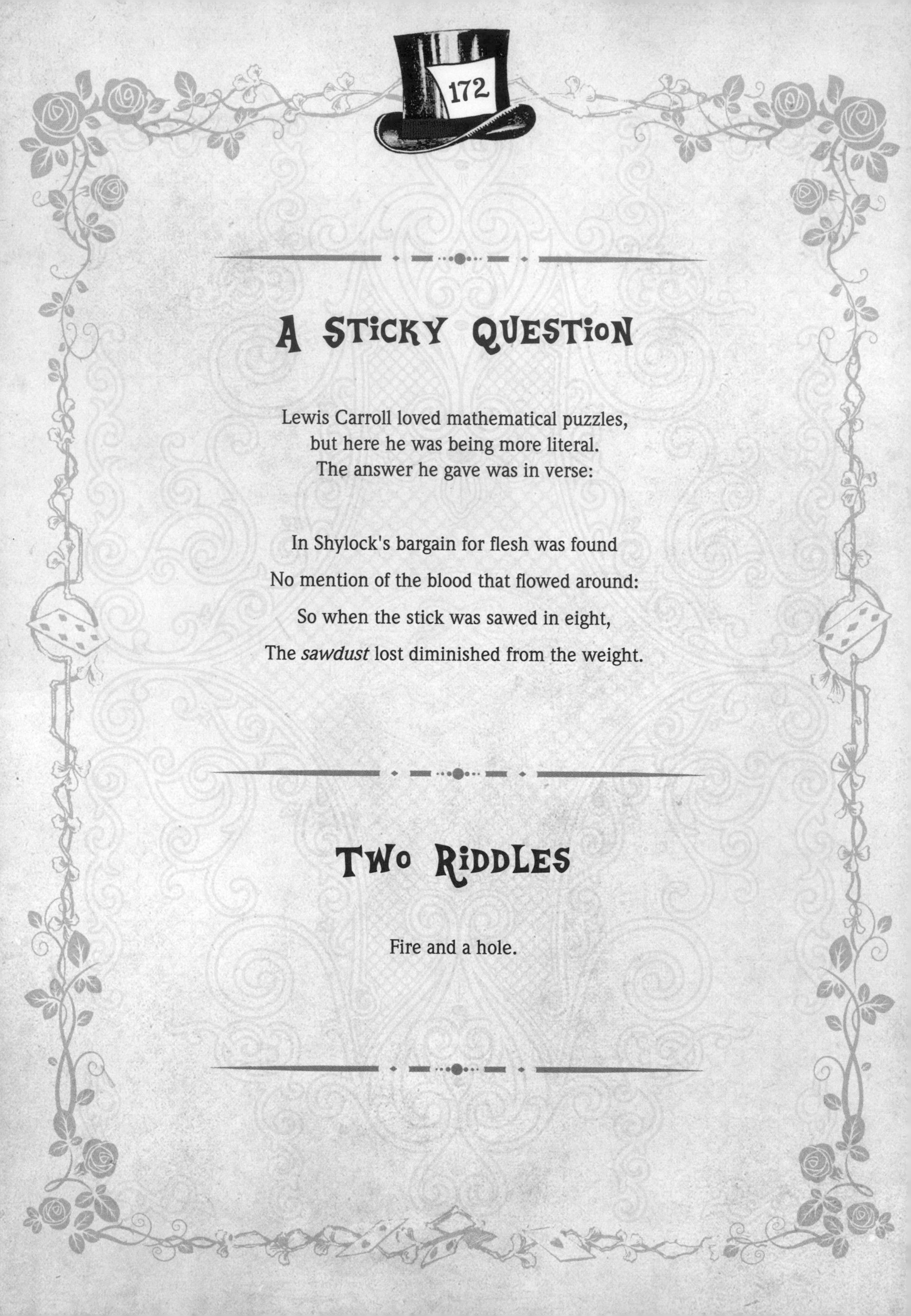

A Sticky Question

Lewis Carroll loved mathematical puzzles, but here he was being more literal. The answer he gave was in verse:

In Shylock's bargain for flesh was found
No mention of the blood that flowed around:
So when the stick was sawed in eight,
The *sawdust* lost diminished from the weight.

Two Riddles

Fire and a hole.

Hat Trick

No chance at all.
There were ten walkers so if nine had located their own hat,
the tenth would also have done so.

MIRROR IMAGE

BALL AND CHAIN

The blacksmith cut all three links on one of the pieces, then used the broken links to join the other three pieces together. He charged six pennies.

PERFORMANCE

Blood, which rushes to your face when you are angry or embarrassed and can be seen in operating theatres.

THE GARDEN OF LIVE FLOWERS

The White Knight's Journey

Yes.

He took as much time for the second half of his trip as the whole trip would have taken on foot. So no matter how fast the horse was, he lost exactly as much time as he spent riding.

He would have saved $\frac{1}{30}$ by walking all the way.

Toasty

He puts two slices of toast in the pan; after 30 seconds he has toasted one side of each. He turns over the first slice, takes the second from the pan, and in its place puts the third slice. After the second half minute the first slice is done and the other two are half done. In the last 30 seconds he finishes the second and third slices.

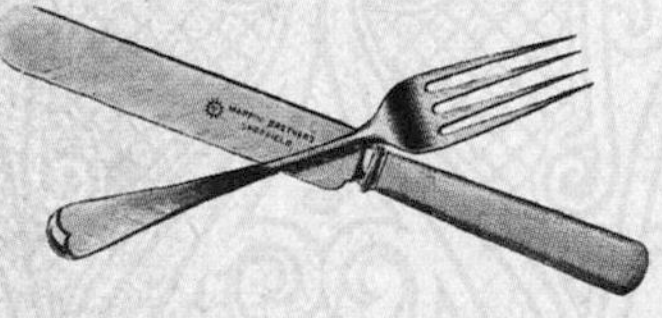

Rose Picking

36 roses.

She gave 20 to the first gardener, leaving her with 16.

To the second she gives 10 leaving her with 6.

And to the third she gave 5 … leaving her with one rose.

SPOT THE DIFFERENCE

A Caucus Race

12 minutes.

Poem

The name of Lewis Carroll's young friend
and the inspiration for the Wonderland books
is hidden in the first letter of each line:

ALICE PLEASANCE LIDDELL

THE CHESHIRE'S CLOCK

An hour and a half, from 12:15 to 1:45. If she hears a single chime seven times in a row, she does not need to wait for it to chime again, for the next cannot be anything but two o'clock.

PEPPER

Alice starts by turning over both the 7-minute and the 11-minute hourglasses. As soon as the sand has stopped running in the 7-minute hourglass, she turns it over again. As soon as the sand has stopped in the 11-minute hourglass, she turns the 7-minute glass again. When the sand has stopped running in the 7-minute hourglass, the 15 minutes will have elapsed.

WHAT'S THE USE?

A coffin.

FOR THE CHOP

Alice said, "I will lose my head."

MIRROR IMAGE
Picture B.
A
C
D

GETTING WARMER

The five temperatures were: -
-2, -1, 1, 2 and 3

-2 x -1 x 1 x 2 x 3 = 12

POOR BOB

Poor Bob was a goldfish.
The dry weather had evaporated the water in his bowl.

TARTS

Alice replied "But that makes no tarts at all, Your Majesty. There are no legs on a snake – and anything multiplied by nothing is nothing."

"Very good," said the Queen, "bring me nothing. Immediately."

2 x 4 x 6 x 2 x 1 x 0 x 3 = 0.

A GAME OF CARDS

Nine. Dum won three games and thus gained three pennies.
Dum has to win back these three pennies, which takes another three games, and then win three more games to win the total of three pennies.

Who Stole the Tarts?

You can solve this by going through each suspect in turn, assuming that they are the thief and checking each statement. For example if we thought the Hatter was the thief then…

The Hatter is *lying*.

The Hare is *lying.*

The Duchess's statement is *true*.

But the Knave's statement is also *true*.

So that cannot be right.

It saves time to look at the one suspect who is talking about herself. If the Duchess were the thief, then…

The Hatter is *lying*.

The Hare is *lying*

The Duchess is *lying*

But the Knave's statement is *true*.

Red pebble

Alice pulled a pebble from the bag and, without looking at it, dropped it onto the ground where it was quickly lost among the others.

"I'm terribly sorry, Your Majesty," said Alice, "but since the other pebble in the bag *must* be the opposite colour, we'll know which one I picked by examining it."

MIRROR IMAGE

Picture C.

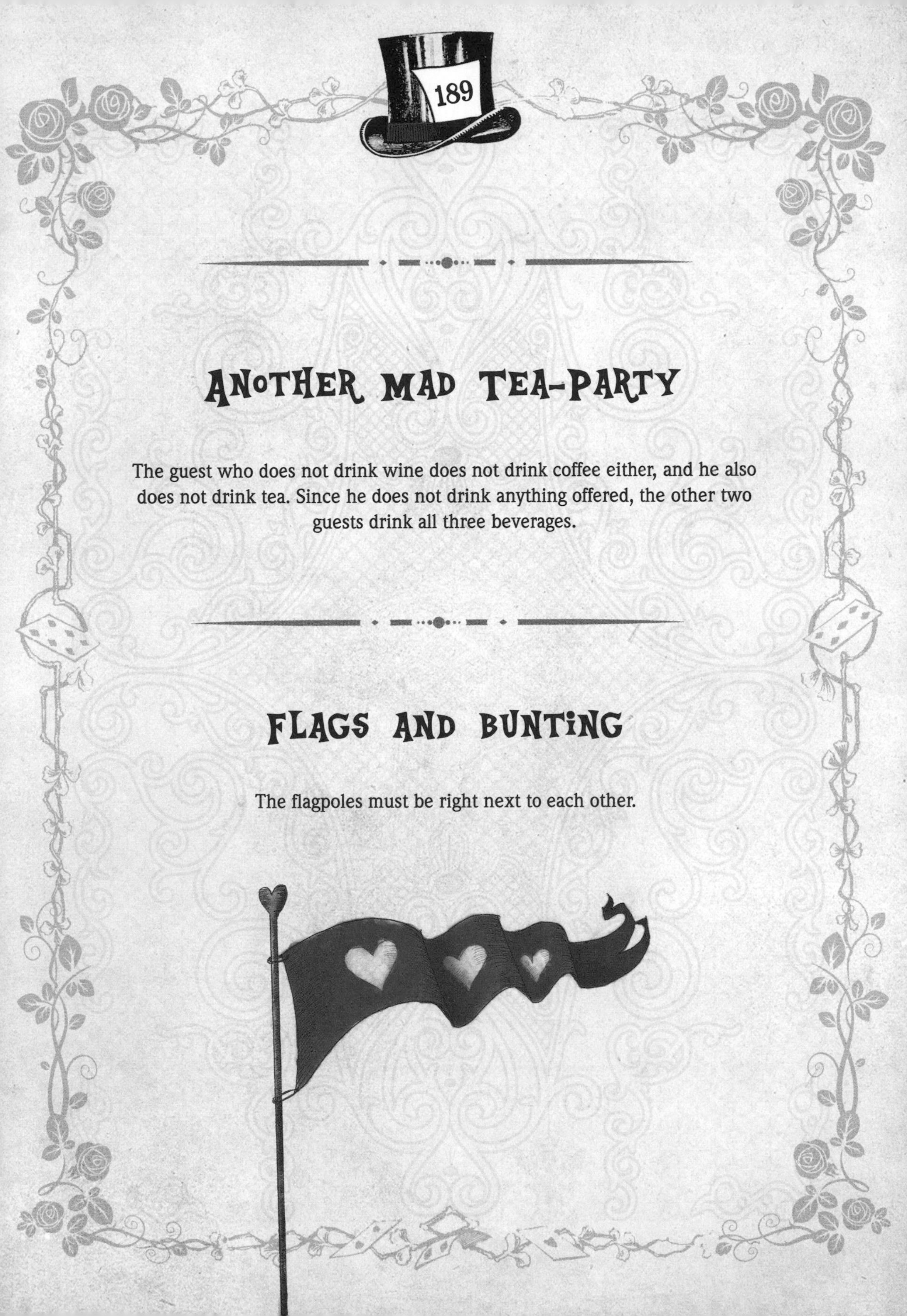

Another Mad Tea-Party

The guest who does not drink wine does not drink coffee either, and he also does not drink tea. Since he does not drink anything offered, the other two guests drink all three beverages.

Flags and Bunting

The flagpoles must be right next to each other.

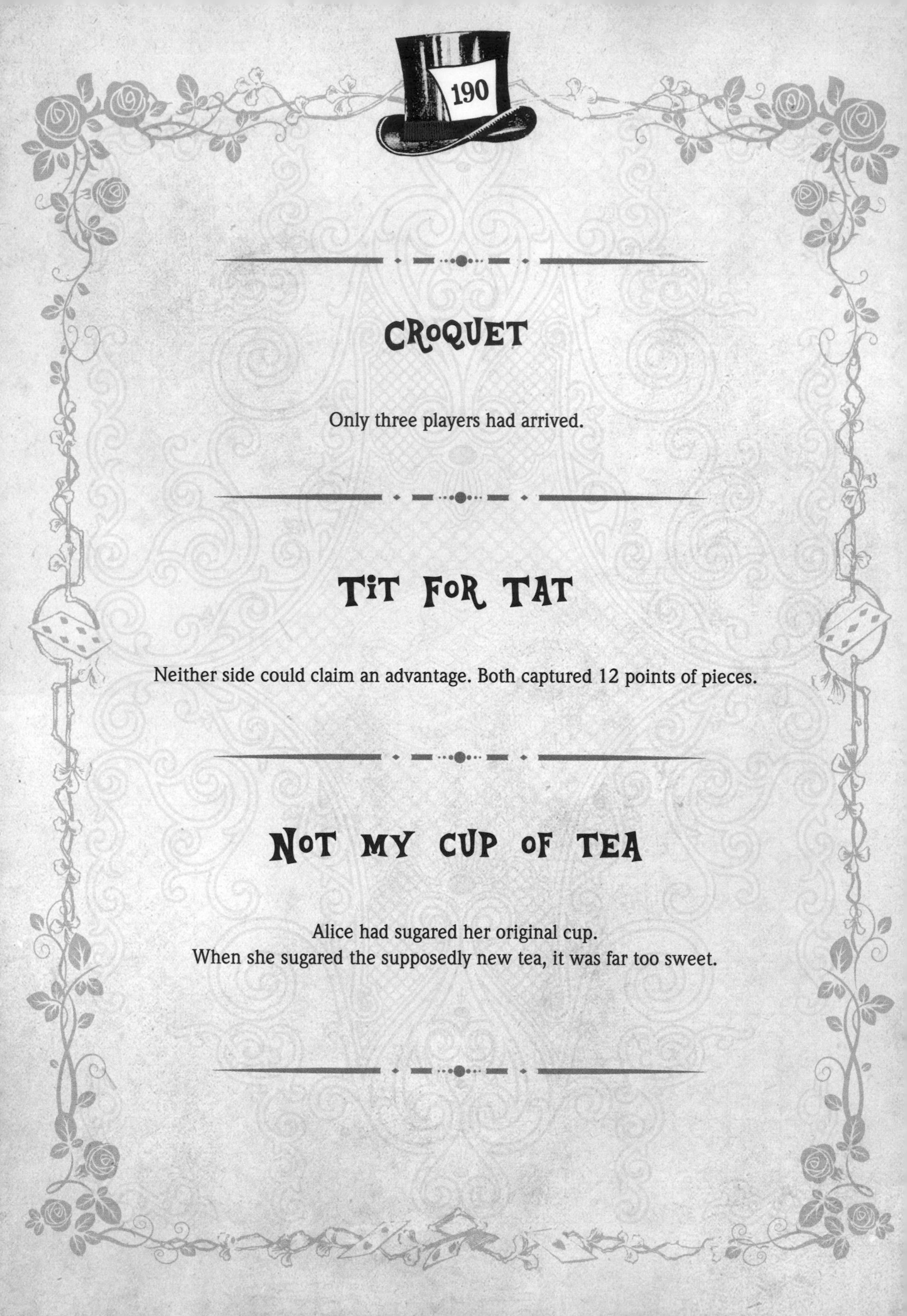

CROQUET

Only three players had arrived.

TIT FOR TAT

Neither side could claim an advantage. Both captured 12 points of pieces.

NOT MY CUP OF TEA

Alice had sugared her original cup.
When she sugared the supposedly new tea, it was far too sweet.

MIRROR IMAGE

Picture D.

A

B

C

E

WHO'S WHO?

Tweedle Dum is on the right and Tweedle Dee is on the left.
If one is lying, the other's statement cannot be true either.

THINK OF A NUMBER

The answer is Three. If you take *any* number and apply the operations of the first verse, they are reversed by the operations of the second.

CURIOUS SOLUTIONS

Clock Watching

When Rabbit left his burrow he wrote down the time it showed (even though he knew it was wrong). When he got to the Hatter's he noted the time when he arrived and the time when he left, so he knew how long he had stayed at the Hatter's. When he got back home, he knew from his own clock how long he had been away from home. Subtracting the time he had spent at the Hatter's, he knew how long the walk back and forth had been. By adding half of this (the time of his return journey) to the time he left the Hatter's, he knew what time it really was.

Letters

Alice could use the looking-glass to determine each letter's symmetry. The four categories were:

Draw 1. Vertical symmetry: A M T U V W Y

Draw 2. Horizontal symmetry: B C D E K

Draw 3. Vertical and horizontal symmetry: H I O X

Draw 4. No symmetry F G J L N P Q R S Z

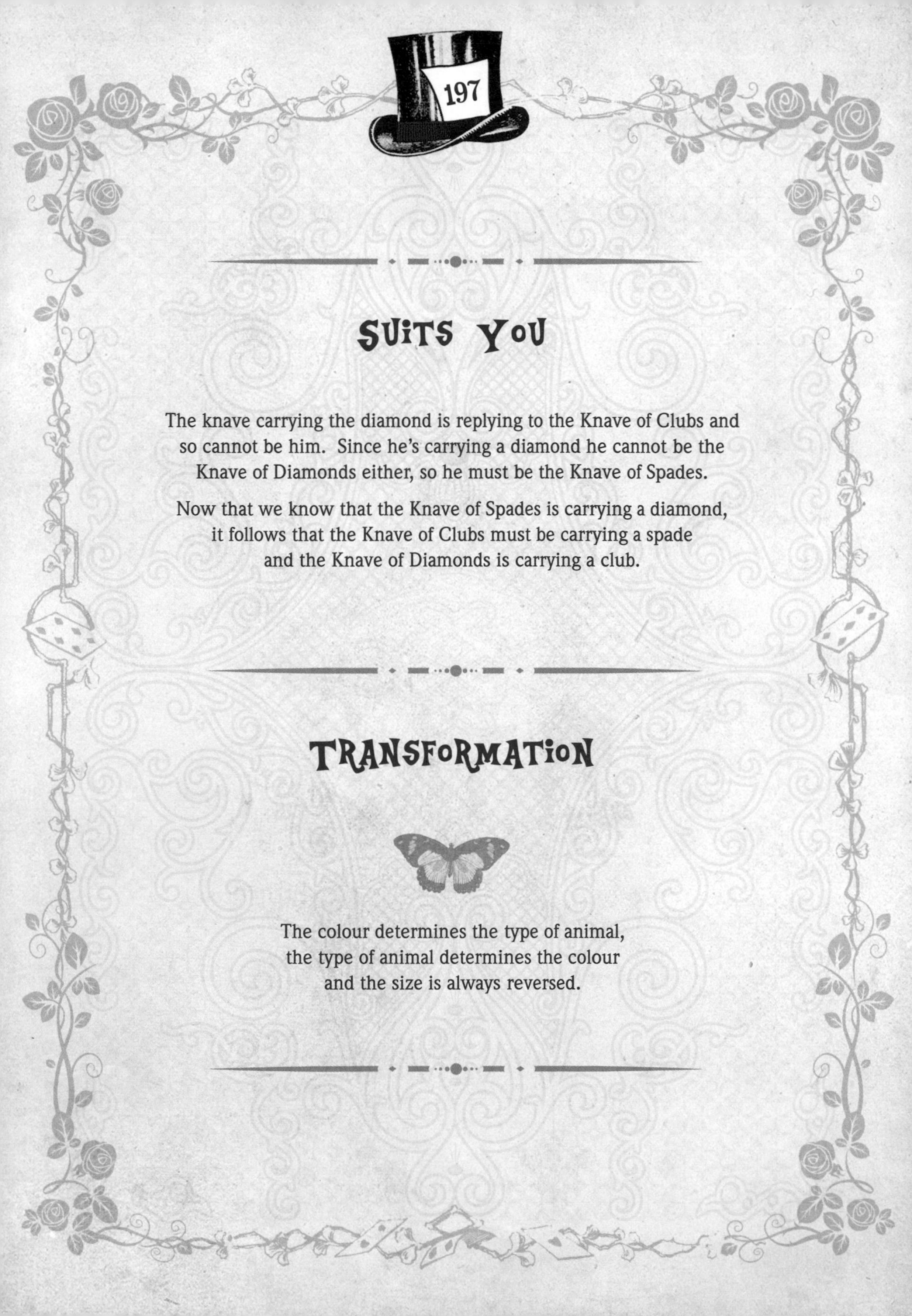

SUITS YOU

The knave carrying the diamond is replying to the Knave of Clubs and so cannot be him. Since he's carrying a diamond he cannot be the Knave of Diamonds either, so he must be the Knave of Spades.

Now that we know that the Knave of Spades is carrying a diamond, it follows that the Knave of Clubs must be carrying a spade and the Knave of Diamonds is carrying a club.

TRANSFORMATION

The colour determines the type of animal, the type of animal determines the colour and the size is always reversed.

SPOT THE DIFFERENCE

Heads and Hats

Alice knew she was wearing a red hat.

The Hatter could not have seen two black hats; otherwise he would have known his was red.

The March Hare (who might be mad but not stupid) realized that the Hatter could not have seen two black hats, so he looked at Alice. Had she been wearing a black hat he would know that his own hat was red. Since this was not the case, Alice's hat must have been red.

Lying Days

The only two days when Lion would make this statement are Monday (lying about Sunday which is a truth day) and Thursday (telling the truth about Wednesday).

Unicorn can only make the statement on a Sunday (telling the truth about Saturday) or Thursday (lying about Wednesday).

So, it must have been a Thursday.

Leaves

If no tree in the wood is completely leafless, then the statement would be true. If there were only two trees for example then both would have just one leaf.

The King's Carriage

For fifty minutes. He saved the carriage ten minutes of travelling time each way and was picked up at 4.50 p.m. rather than the usual time.

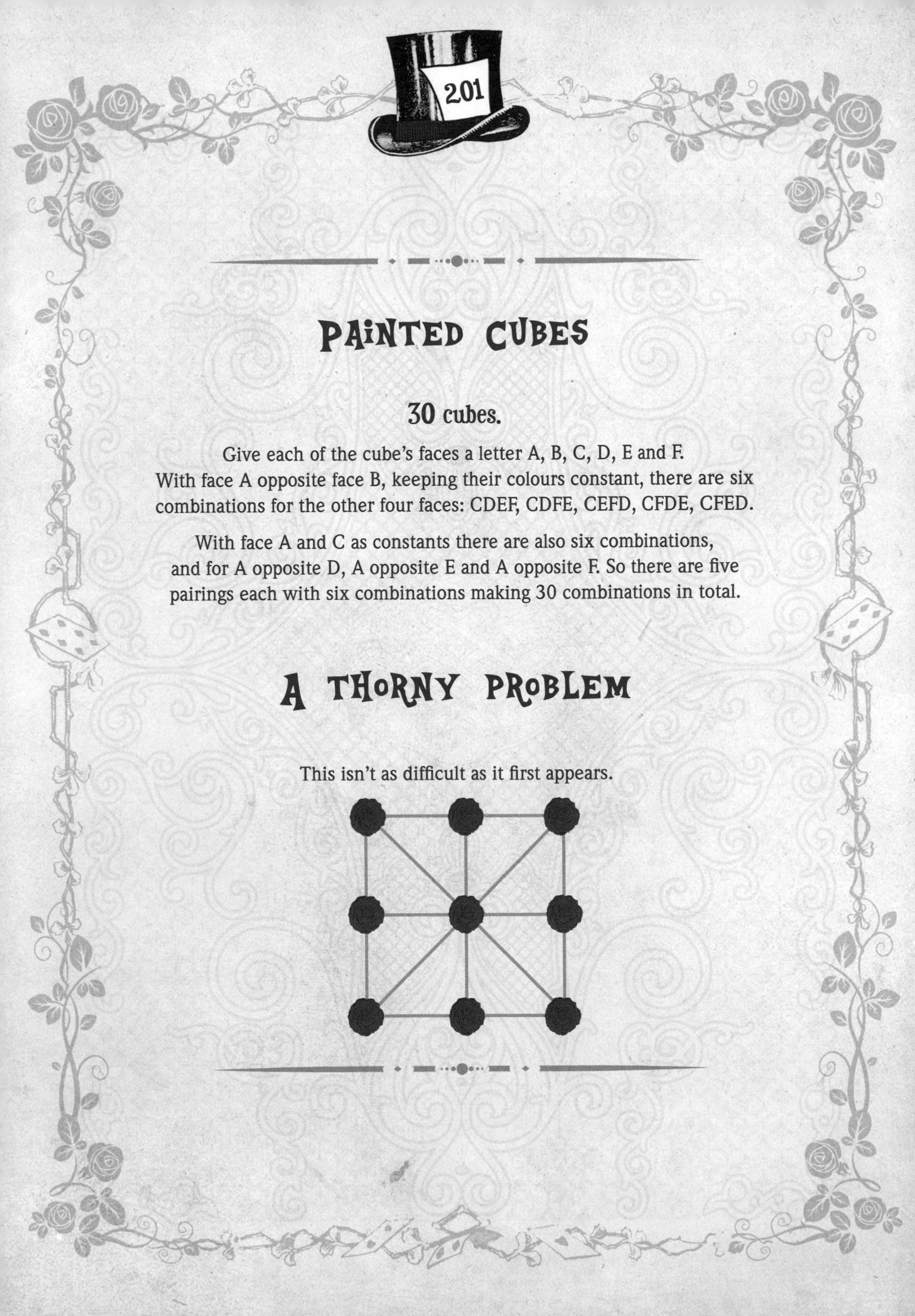

PAINTED CUBES

30 cubes.

Give each of the cube's faces a letter A, B, C, D, E and F. With face A opposite face B, keeping their colours constant, there are six combinations for the other four faces: CDEF, CDFE, CEFD, CFDE, CFED.

With face A and C as constants there are also six combinations, and for A opposite D, A opposite E and A opposite F. So there are five pairings each with six combinations making 30 combinations in total.

A THORNY PROBLEM

This isn't as difficult as it first appears.

SPOT THE DIFFERENCE

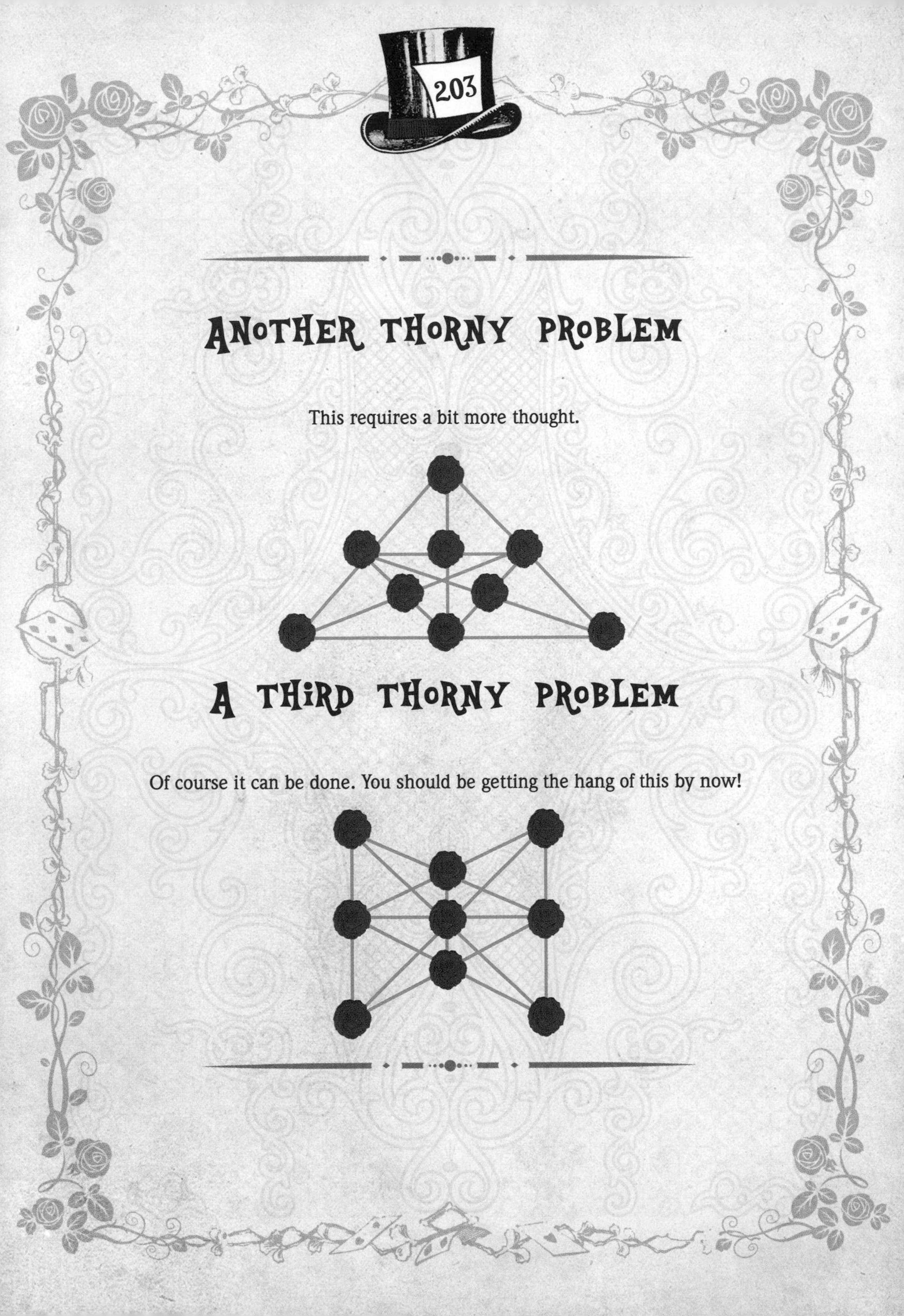

ANOTHER THORNY PROBLEM

This requires a bit more thought.

A THIRD THORNY PROBLEM

Of course it can be done. You should be getting the hang of this by now!

A Head Start

We know from the first race that Alice runs 100 yards in the same time as the Dodo runs 95 yards. It follows, therefore, that in the second race both would be neck and neck 5 yards short of the finishing line. As Alice is the faster runner she would overtake the Dodo in the last 5 yards and win the second race.

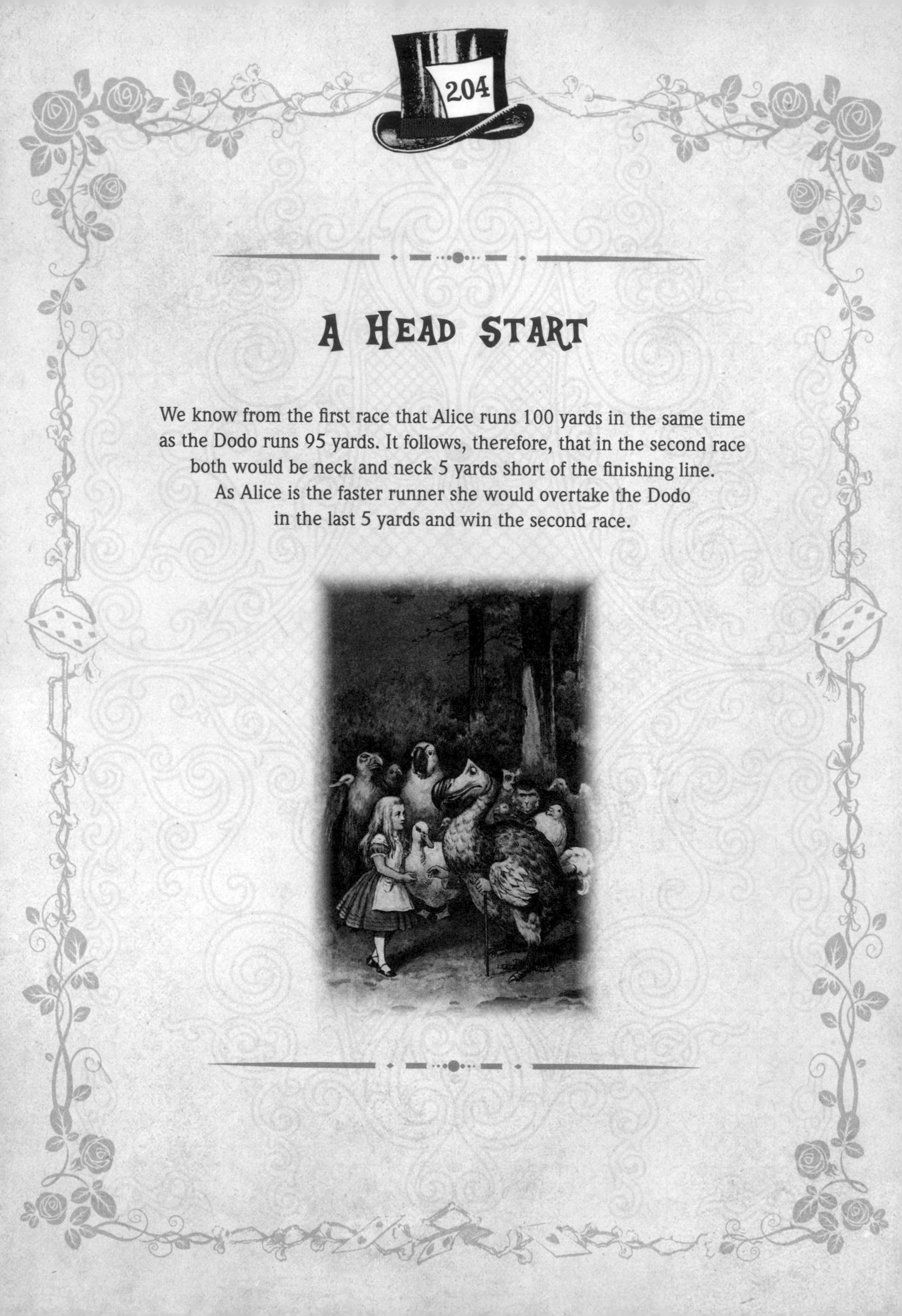

Hide & Seek

If we number the gardeners 1 to 4, we can list all the possible combinations of two cards that Alice might pick like so:

1-2	2-3	3-4	4-KS	KS-KH
1-3	2-4	3-KS	4-KH	
1-4	2-KS	3-KH		
1-KS	2-KH			
1-KH				

The knaves appear in 9 out of the 15 pairs. So the chances of Alice picking at least one knave is $\frac{9}{15}$ or 60 per cent. This is better than an even chance (50 per cent) so the odds are slightly in Alice's favour.

Eyes of the Wise

He had to keep 16 Wise Men.

SPOT THE DIFFERENCE

STAMPS

You must use the 4d stamp twice, placing it on the same square as the ½d stamp as shown. Each row, column and diagonal then totals 9d.

2d	5d	1d
2d	3d	4d
4d	1	3d

THREE CARDS

Ace of Diamonds, King of Hearts, Two of Spades.

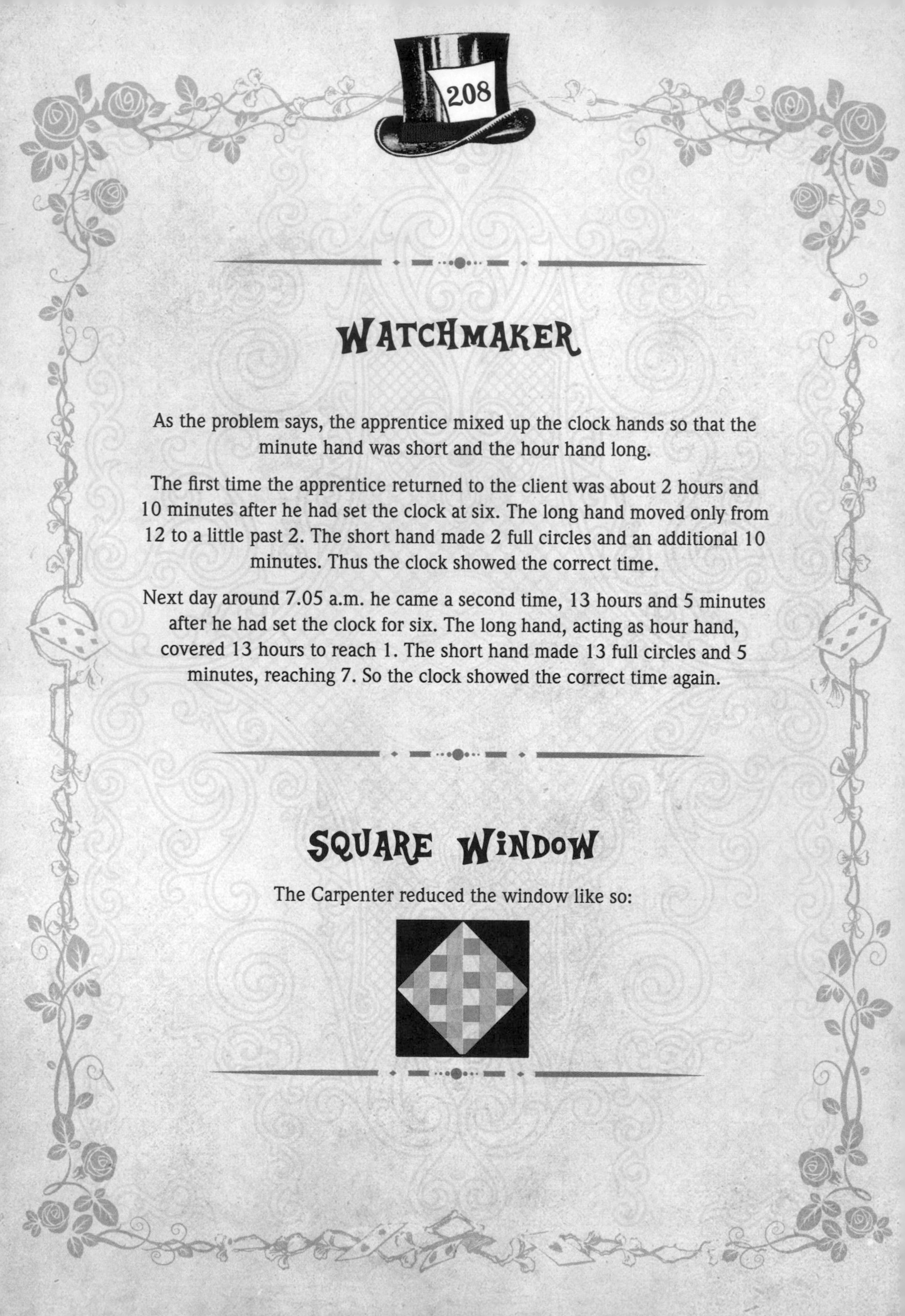

WATCHMAKER

As the problem says, the apprentice mixed up the clock hands so that the minute hand was short and the hour hand long.

The first time the apprentice returned to the client was about 2 hours and 10 minutes after he had set the clock at six. The long hand moved only from 12 to a little past 2. The short hand made 2 full circles and an additional 10 minutes. Thus the clock showed the correct time.

Next day around 7.05 a.m. he came a second time, 13 hours and 5 minutes after he had set the clock for six. The long hand, acting as hour hand, covered 13 hours to reach 1. The short hand made 13 full circles and 5 minutes, reaching 7. So the clock showed the correct time again.

SQUARE WINDOW

The Carpenter reduced the window like so:

MIRROR IMAGE

Picture B.

A

C

D

CAKES ON A TRAIN

Most people immediately answer that one took three coins and the other five but this is incorrect.

The 8 coins was in payment for a third of eight cakes, which is $2\frac{2}{3}$ cakes ($\frac{8}{3}$).

From this we can say that the value of all eight cakes is 24 coins and that a single cake is worth 3.

Since each ended up with $2\frac{2}{3}$ cakes, the first passenger, who had three cakes to start with, gave $\frac{1}{3}$ of a cake to Alice; the other $2\frac{1}{3}$ was given by the other passenger.

Therefore, 1 coin goes to the first passenger and 7 to the second.

WORTH THE WEIGHT

1 pound, 3 pounds, 9 pounds.

The sheep can put any combination of weights on either pan and the difference between the two weights is the amount of sweets she sells. The weight required is the result of an addition or subtraction sum.

$1 - 0 = 1$

$3 - 1 = 2$

$3 - 0 = 3$

$(3 + 1) - 0 = 4$

$9 - (3 + 1) = 5$

$9 - 3 = 6$

$(9 + 1) - 3 = 7$

$9 - 1 = 8$

$9 - 0 = 9$

$(9 + 1) - 0 = 10$

$(9 + 3) - 1 = 11$

$(9 + 3) - 0 = 12$

and finally

$(9 + 3 + 1) - 0 = 13$

YOU ARE OLD, FATHER WILLIAM

It is possible if the statement was made on 1st January. Father William's birthday is 31st December. He was 67 the day before yesterday. He was 68 yesterday, his birthday. He will be 69 this year, and 70 next year.

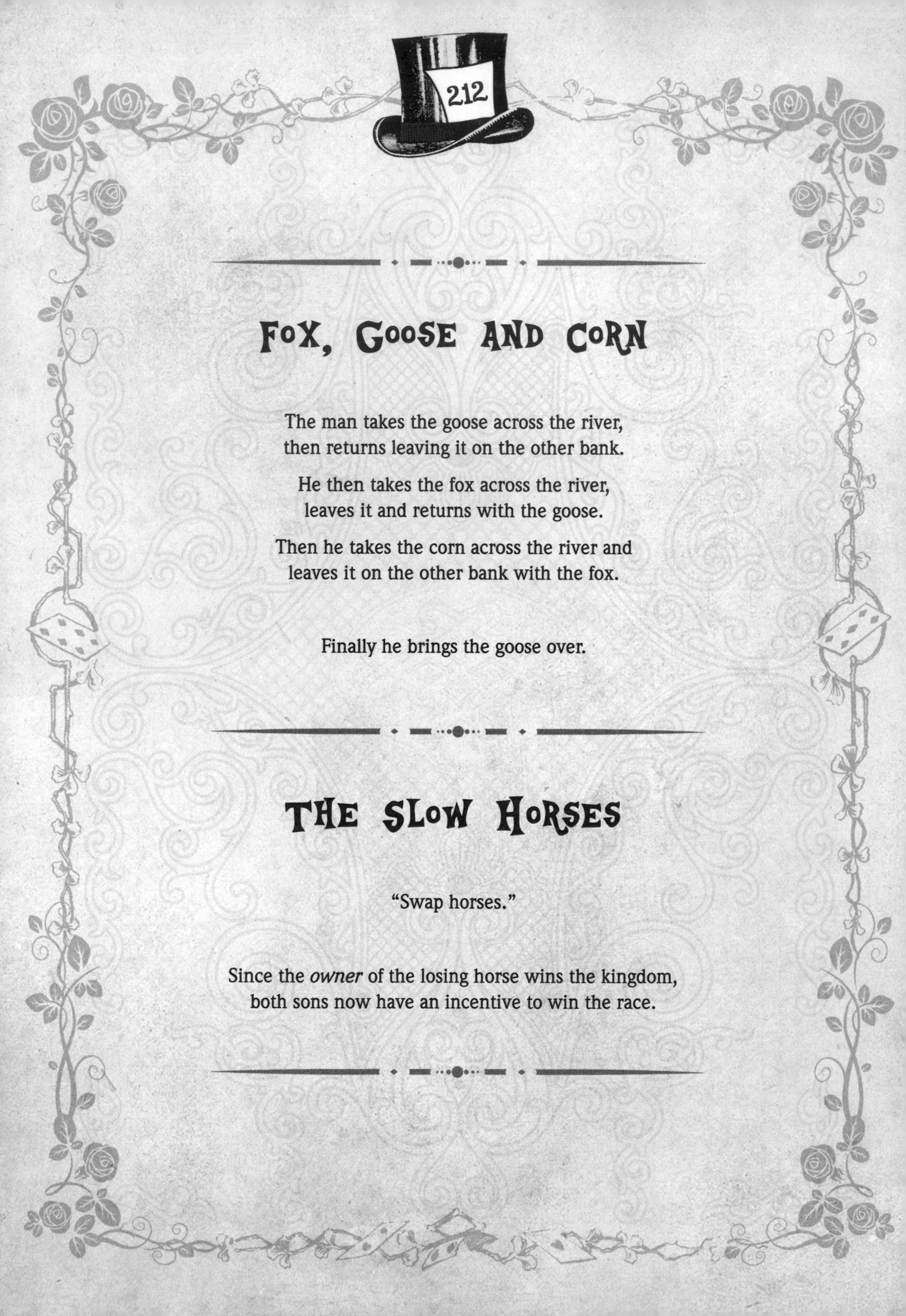

Fox, Goose and Corn

The man takes the goose across the river, then returns leaving it on the other bank.

He then takes the fox across the river, leaves it and returns with the goose.

Then he takes the corn across the river and leaves it on the other bank with the fox.

Finally he brings the goose over.

The Slow Horses

"Swap horses."

Since the *owner* of the losing horse wins the kingdom, both sons now have an incentive to win the race.

SPOT THE DIFFERENCE

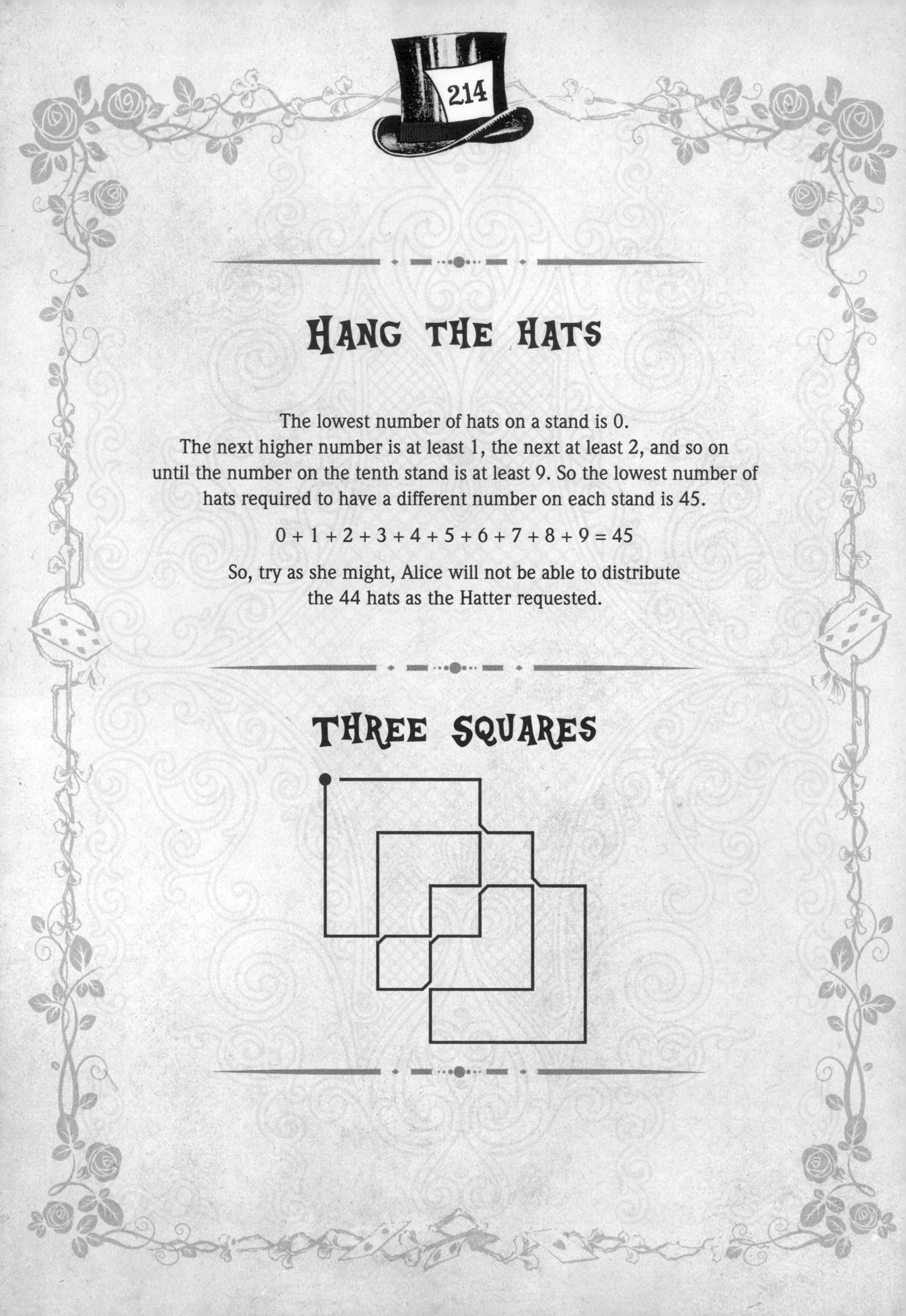

Hang the Hats

The lowest number of hats on a stand is 0.
The next higher number is at least 1, the next at least 2, and so on until the number on the tenth stand is at least 9. So the lowest number of hats required to have a different number on each stand is 45.

$$0 + 1 + 2 + 3 + 4 + 5 + 6 + 7 + 8 + 9 = 45$$

So, try as she might, Alice will not be able to distribute the 44 hats as the Hatter requested.

Three Squares

A Knight on the Town

Two round trips made the first way would take 3 hours, thus covering the distance between home and office twice walking and twice riding. So the Knight could make the round trip by walking in 3 hours minus a half, or 2½ hours.

Hat Pins

The ten cushions should contain the following numbers of pins:

1, 2, 4, 8, 16, 32, 64, 128, 256, 489.

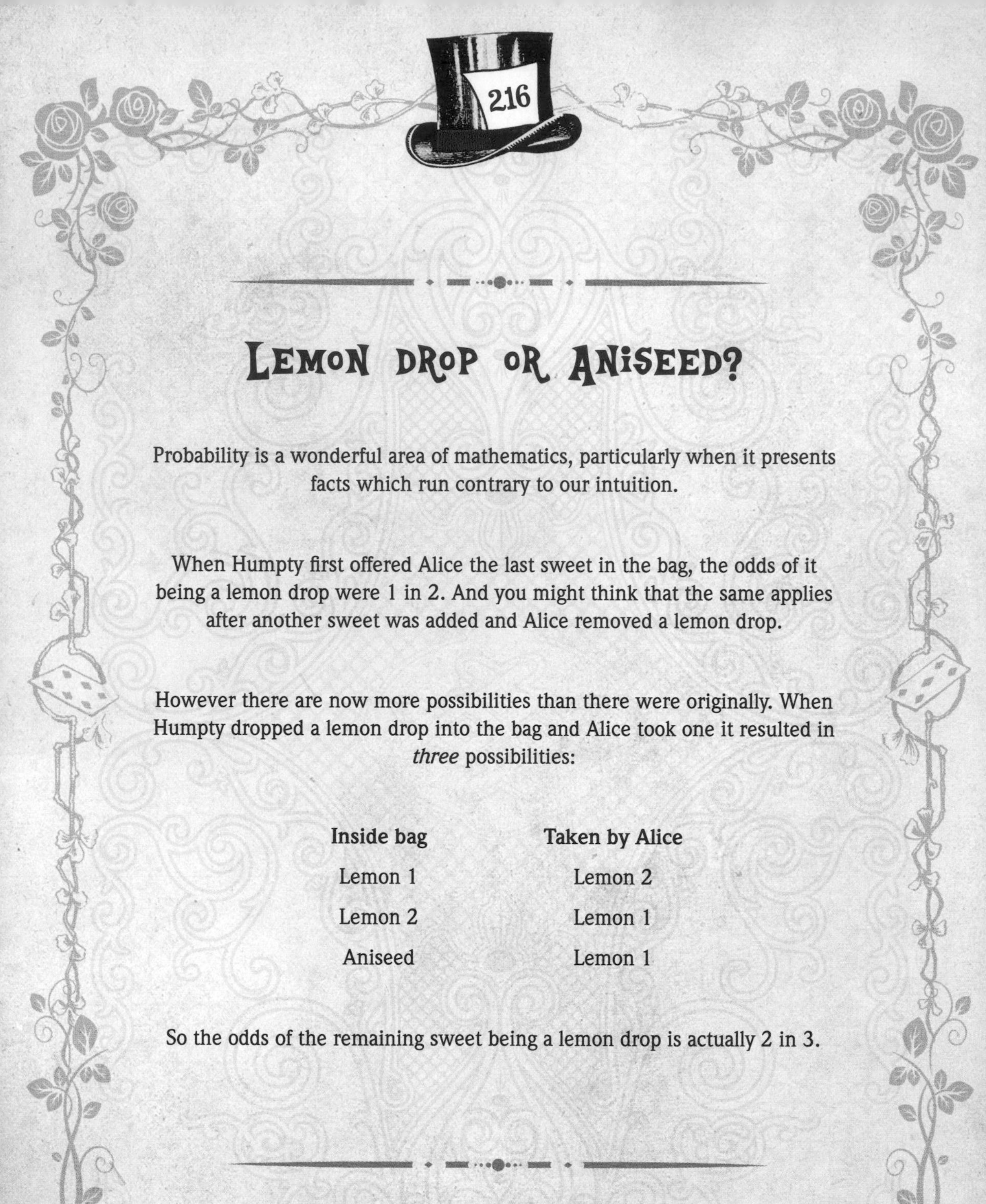

LEMON DROP OR ANISEED?

Probability is a wonderful area of mathematics, particularly when it presents facts which run contrary to our intuition.

When Humpty first offered Alice the last sweet in the bag, the odds of it being a lemon drop were 1 in 2. And you might think that the same applies after another sweet was added and Alice removed a lemon drop.

However there are now more possibilities than there were originally. When Humpty dropped a lemon drop into the bag and Alice took one it resulted in *three* possibilities:

Inside bag	**Taken by Alice**
Lemon 1	Lemon 2
Lemon 2	Lemon 1
Aniseed	Lemon 1

So the odds of the remaining sweet being a lemon drop is actually 2 in 3.

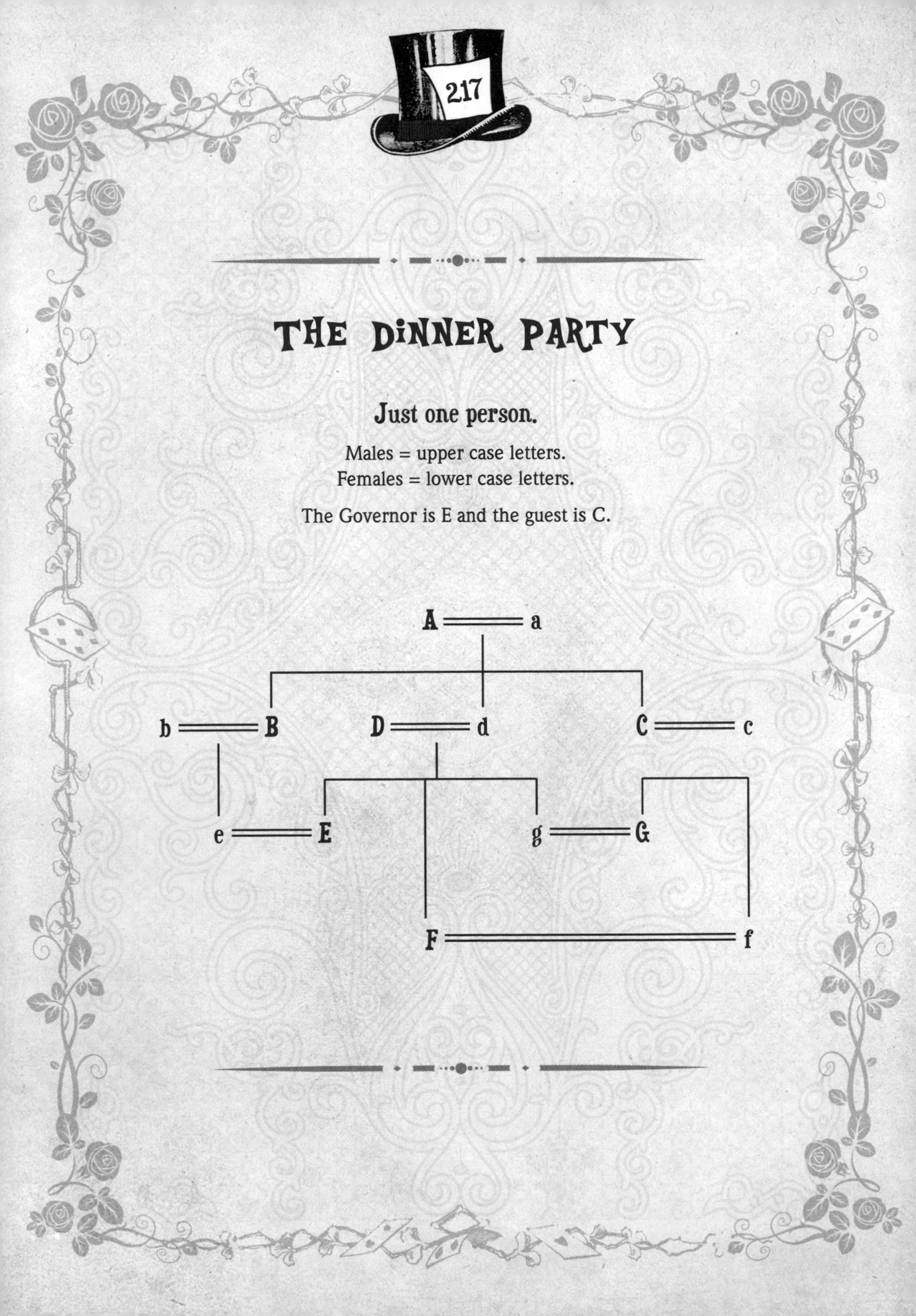

THE DINNER PARTY

Just one person.

Males = upper case letters.
Females = lower case letters.

The Governor is E and the guest is C.

Fifty Pounds

Since the same counterfeit note was used
in all the transactions, they are all invalid.

Everyone's debts are where they were before the Hatter picked up the note.
The exception is the butcher who owes £50 to the farmer for the pig.

ALL THE KING'S MEN

Deducting ten leaves 90 soldiers who are proficient in something.

83 are proficient horse-riders,
leaving seven who could only be good at marksmanship.
Deduct these from 75 and there remains 68 who were skilled at both.

SWEETS

There are six possible sweet combinations:

RED+RED	RED(1)+WHITE
RED(2)+WHITE	RED(1)+BLUE
RED(2)+BLUE	WHITE+BLUE

Alice knows that the WHITE+BLUE combination has not been drawn. That leaves five possible combinations, so the chance that the RED+RED pairing has been drawn is 1 in 5.

GREAT WALL

Fifty-eight minutes.
His total progress each minute is one foot, but he reaches the top of the wall on the fifty-eighth minute before he would normally slip back two feet.

A ROYAL PREDICAMENT

Alice could ask either Queen:
"What would the other Queen say if I asked her which looking-glass will send me home?"

This question will get the same answer from both Queens.

The truthful Queen would have to tell Alice the lying Queen's answer – a lie.

The lying Queen would give the opposite of the truthful Queen's answer – a lie.

So if Alice asked either Queen the question, they would both point to the looking-glass that she should not take.

WHO ARE YOU?

A	L	I	C	E
C	E	A	L	I
L	I	C	E	A
E	A	L	I	C
I	C	E	A	L

HARDER SOLUTIONS

MULTIPLICATION

Alice's four times table seems like nonsense, except that the answers go up by one each time.

However, if her answers are converted to different *number bases*, we see a pattern.

	(base 10)	in base	is...	
4 x 3 =	12	12	10	
4 x 4 =	16	15	11	
4 x 5 =	20	18	12	
4 x 6 =	24	21	13	
4 x 7 =	28	24	14	
4 x 8 =	32	27	15	
4 x 9 =	36	30	16	
4 x 10 =	40	33	17	
4 x 11 =	44	36	18	
4 x 12 =	48	39	19	

She cannot reach 20 following this pattern because:

4 x 13 =	52	42	1A	(not 20)

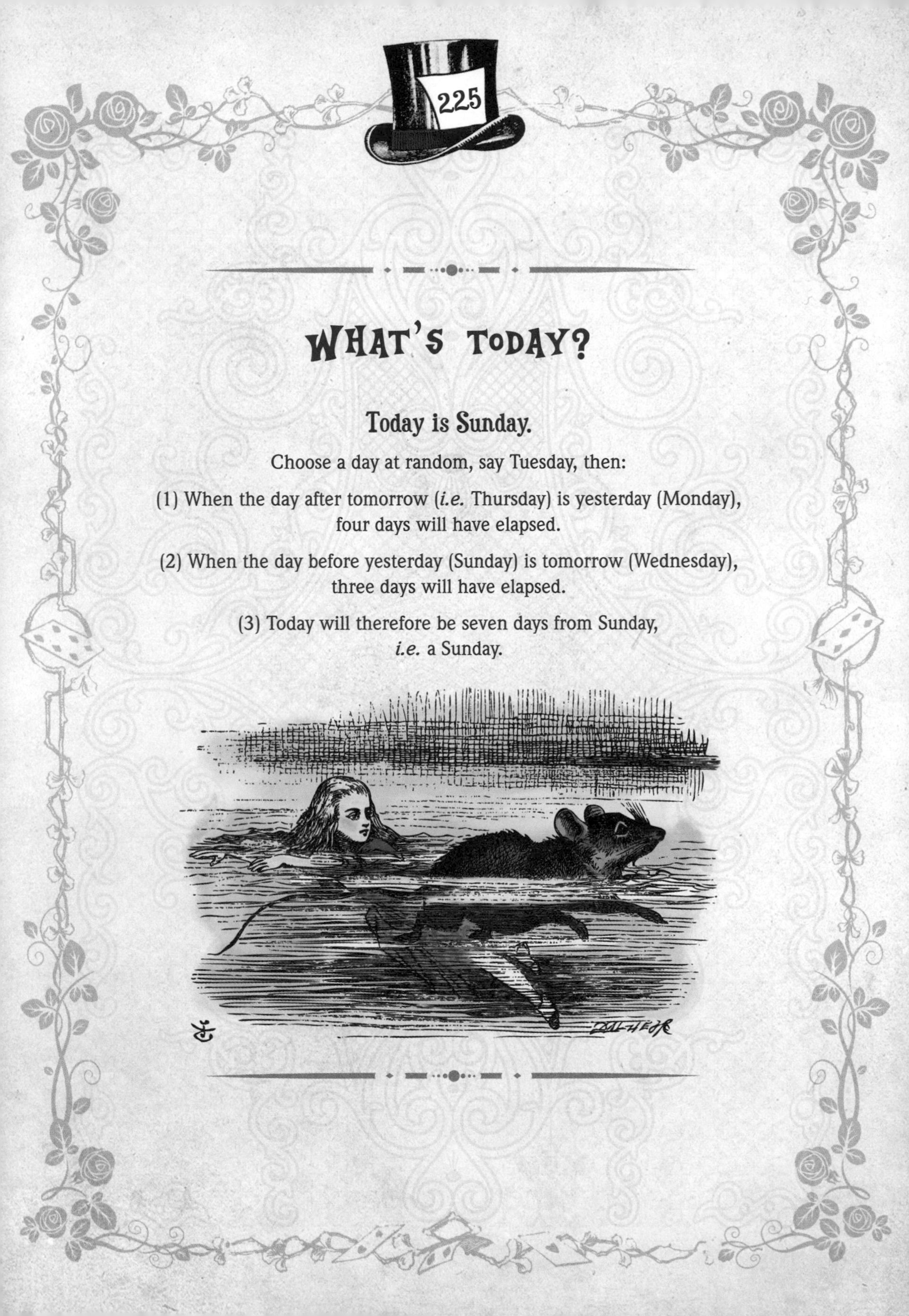

WHAT'S TODAY?

Today is Sunday.

Choose a day at random, say Tuesday, then:

(1) When the day after tomorrow (*i.e.* Thursday) is yesterday (Monday), four days will have elapsed.

(2) When the day before yesterday (Sunday) is tomorrow (Wednesday), three days will have elapsed.

(3) Today will therefore be seven days from Sunday, *i.e.* a Sunday.

SPOT THE DIFFERENCE

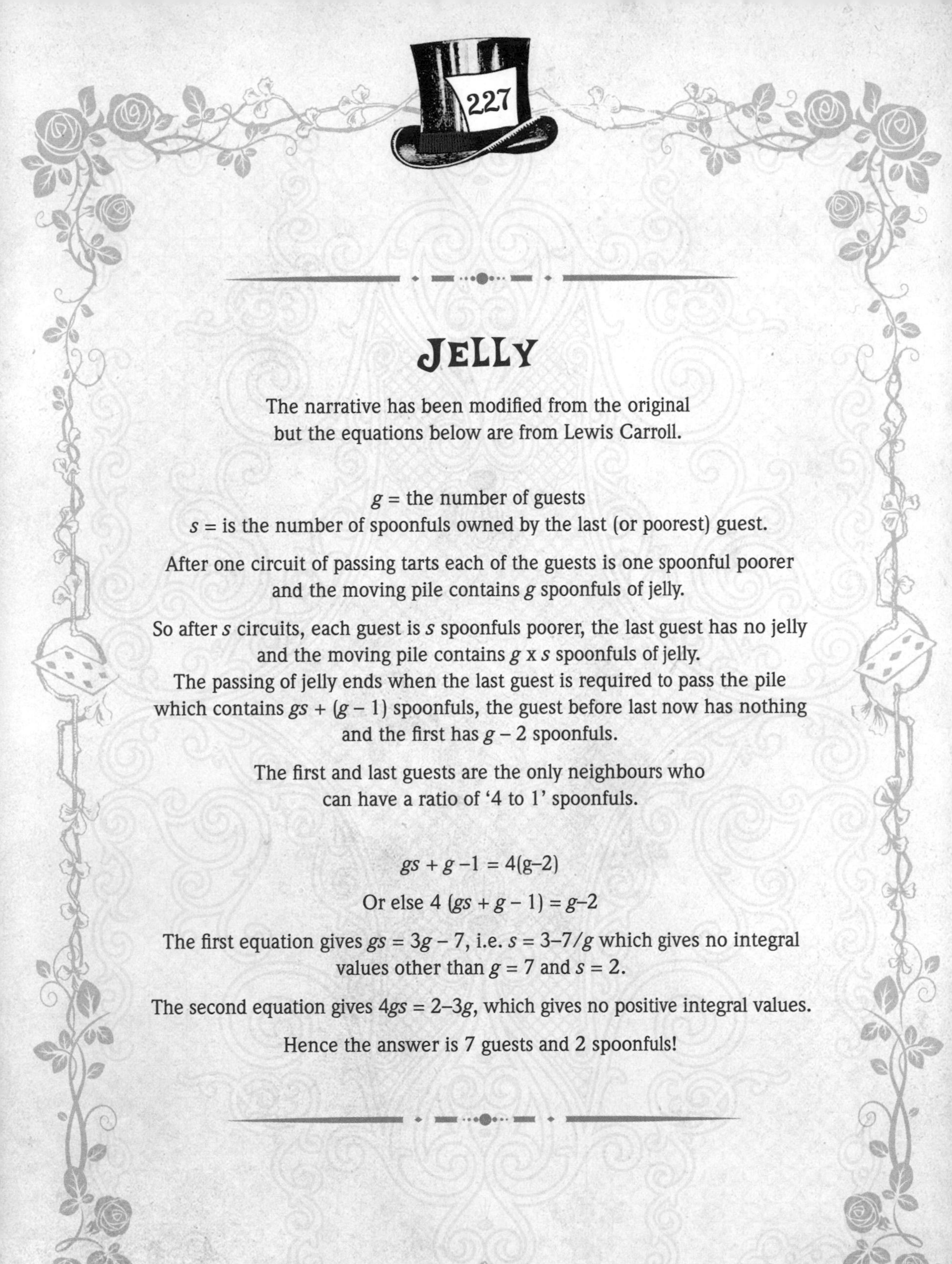

JELLY

The narrative has been modified from the original
but the equations below are from Lewis Carroll.

g = the number of guests
s = is the number of spoonfuls owned by the last (or poorest) guest.

After one circuit of passing tarts each of the guests is one spoonful poorer and the moving pile contains g spoonfuls of jelly.

So after s circuits, each guest is s spoonfuls poorer, the last guest has no jelly and the moving pile contains $g \times s$ spoonfuls of jelly.
The passing of jelly ends when the last guest is required to pass the pile which contains $gs + (g - 1)$ spoonfuls, the guest before last now has nothing and the first has $g - 2$ spoonfuls.

The first and last guests are the only neighbours who can have a ratio of '4 to 1' spoonfuls.

$$gs + g - 1 = 4(g-2)$$

Or else $4(gs + g - 1) = g-2$

The first equation gives $gs = 3g - 7$, i.e. $s = 3-7/g$ which gives no integral values other than $g = 7$ and $s = 2$.

The second equation gives $4gs = 2-3g$, which gives no positive integral values.

Hence the answer is 7 guests and 2 spoonfuls!

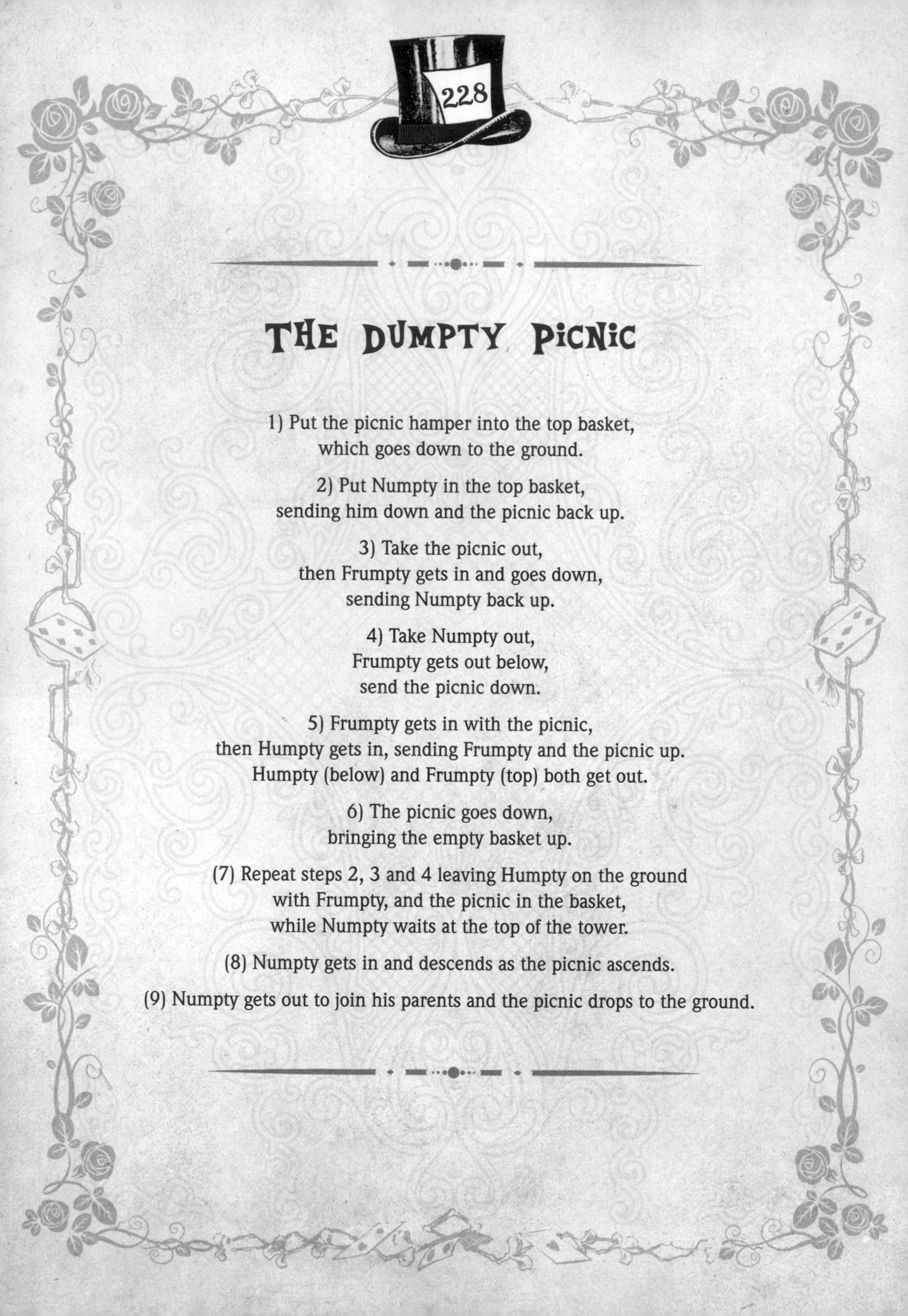

THE DUMPTY PICNIC

1) Put the picnic hamper into the top basket,
which goes down to the ground.

2) Put Numpty in the top basket,
sending him down and the picnic back up.

3) Take the picnic out,
then Frumpty gets in and goes down,
sending Numpty back up.

4) Take Numpty out,
Frumpty gets out below,
send the picnic down.

5) Frumpty gets in with the picnic,
then Humpty gets in, sending Frumpty and the picnic up.
Humpty (below) and Frumpty (top) both get out.

6) The picnic goes down,
bringing the empty basket up.

(7) Repeat steps 2, 3 and 4 leaving Humpty on the ground
with Frumpty, and the picnic in the basket,
while Numpty waits at the top of the tower.

(8) Numpty gets in and descends as the picnic ascends.

(9) Numpty gets out to join his parents and the picnic drops to the ground.

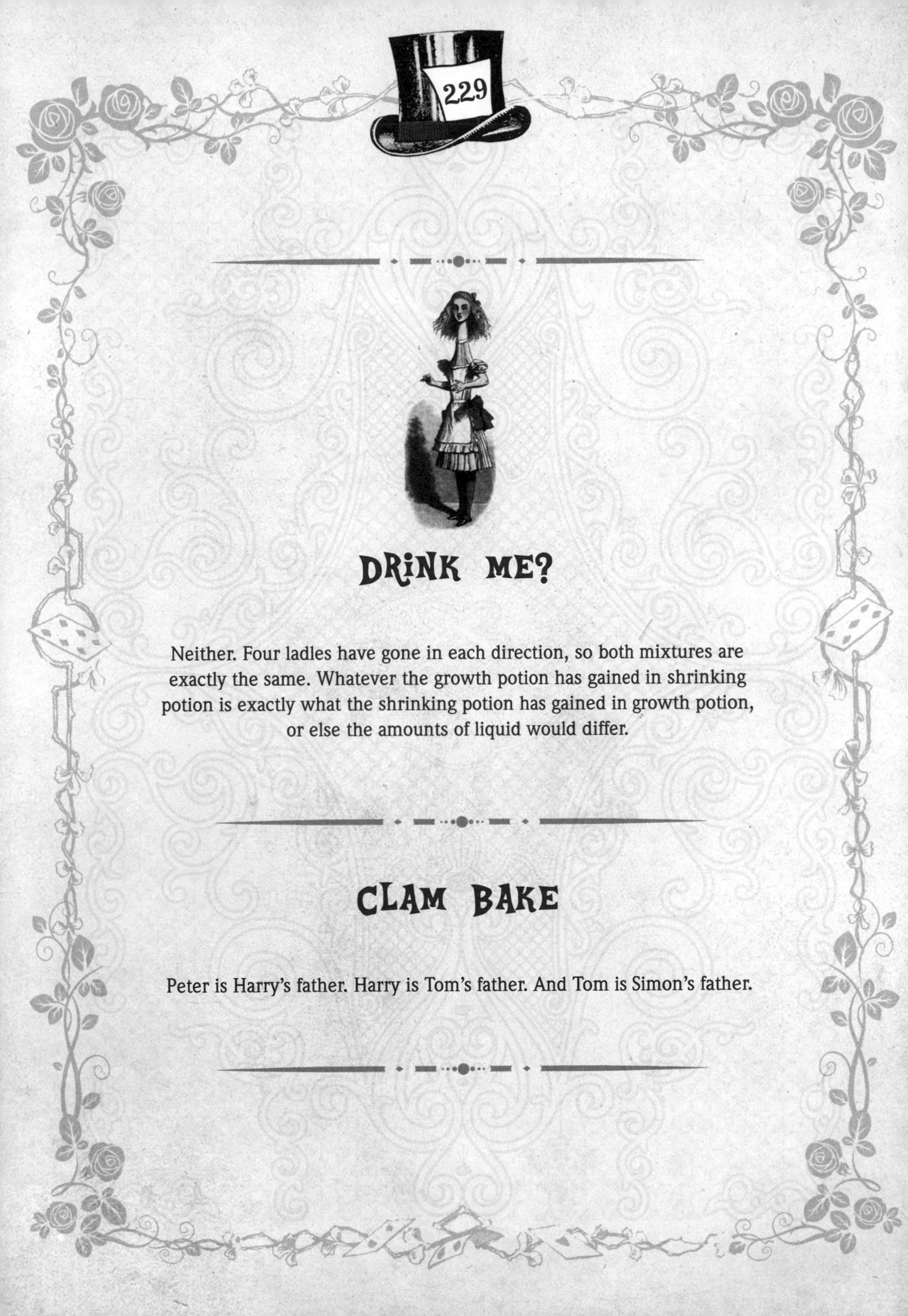

DRINK ME?

Neither. Four ladles have gone in each direction, so both mixtures are exactly the same. Whatever the growth potion has gained in shrinking potion is exactly what the shrinking potion has gained in growth potion, or else the amounts of liquid would differ.

CLAM BAKE

Peter is Harry's father. Harry is Tom's father. And Tom is Simon's father.

SPOT THE DIFFERENCE

Royal Scandal

The King was a widower. After his first wife died, he married her sister. His death left his second wife a widow, meaning that his first wife became his widow's sister.

The Queen's Garden

88 x 88.5 yards.

The length of the path in yards is equal to the area of the garden. Although the length and width are uneven, taking the square root of the area (88.249...) gives an estimate of the value mid-way between them. Since we know the difference is 0.5 yards, we can confirm that 88 and 88.5 are the correct values.

THE LION AND THE UNICORN

The Unicorn is 16 years old.

Take the two ages: the Lion 'now' (*L*) and the Unicorn 'in the past' (*U*).

We don't know how much older the Lion is but we'll assign it the letter *Y* so we can convert the Unicorn's statement into an equation:

$$L / 2 + Y = 1/2 \times 3 \times 3 \times U.$$

Multiplying that by 2 gives L + 2Y = 9U, which means the Lion now + twice their age gap is equal to nine times Unicorn in the past.

We know that 'in the past', the Lion was three times the Unicorn's age, so the gap was (and always is) twice the Unicorn's age 'in the past'; or Y = 2U.

So L + 4U = 9U, or L = 5U. The Lion is five times as old now as the Unicorn was when the Lion was 3 times as old as the Unicorn, and since the gap is 2U, the Unicorn's age now is 5U – 2U = 3U. So the current ratio of their ages is 5:3. We know the total is 44, so 5U + 3U = 44.

That means U = 44/8 = 5.5, the age of the Unicorn 'in the past'. So L (the Lion 'now') is 5.5x5 = 27.5, and Unicorn's age now is 5.5x3 = 16.5.

BLIND DEREK

The only combination of chests and contents for which the first two pirates could easily infer the colour of their third coin while the third pirate could not is as follows:

Chest	1	2	3	4
Label	*G G S*	*G S S*	*G G G*	*S S S*
Contents	G G G	G G S	S S S	G S S

Blind Derek came to his conclusion like so:

1. If Colin, having drawn S S, cannot tell the colour of the third coin, the label must be marked *GGG.*

2. If Albert, having drawn BB, knows the colour of the third coin, then the label must be marked *BBW* or *BBB*. However, as *BBB* is already identified as belonging to Colin, Albert's label must be *BBW*.

3. Barney, having drawn WB and knowing the colour of the remaining coin, could have labels marked BWW or BBW. However, BBW is eliminated by (2); therefore his label is marked BWW.

4. Finally, the only combination remaining for Blind Derek is a label marked WWW, with contents of BWW.

SPOT THE DIFFERENCE

River Madness

Because the rate of flow of the river has the same effect on both the boat and the hat, it can be ignored. Instead of the water moving and the shore remaining fixed, imagine the water as perfectly still and the shore moving. As far as the boat and the hat are concerned, this situation is exactly the same as before. Since the Hatter rows 5 miles away from the hat, then 5 miles back, he has rowed a total distance of 10 miles with respect to the water. Since his rowing speed with respect to the water is 5 miles an hour, it must have taken him 2 hours to go the 10 miles. He would therefore recover his hat at 4 o'clock.

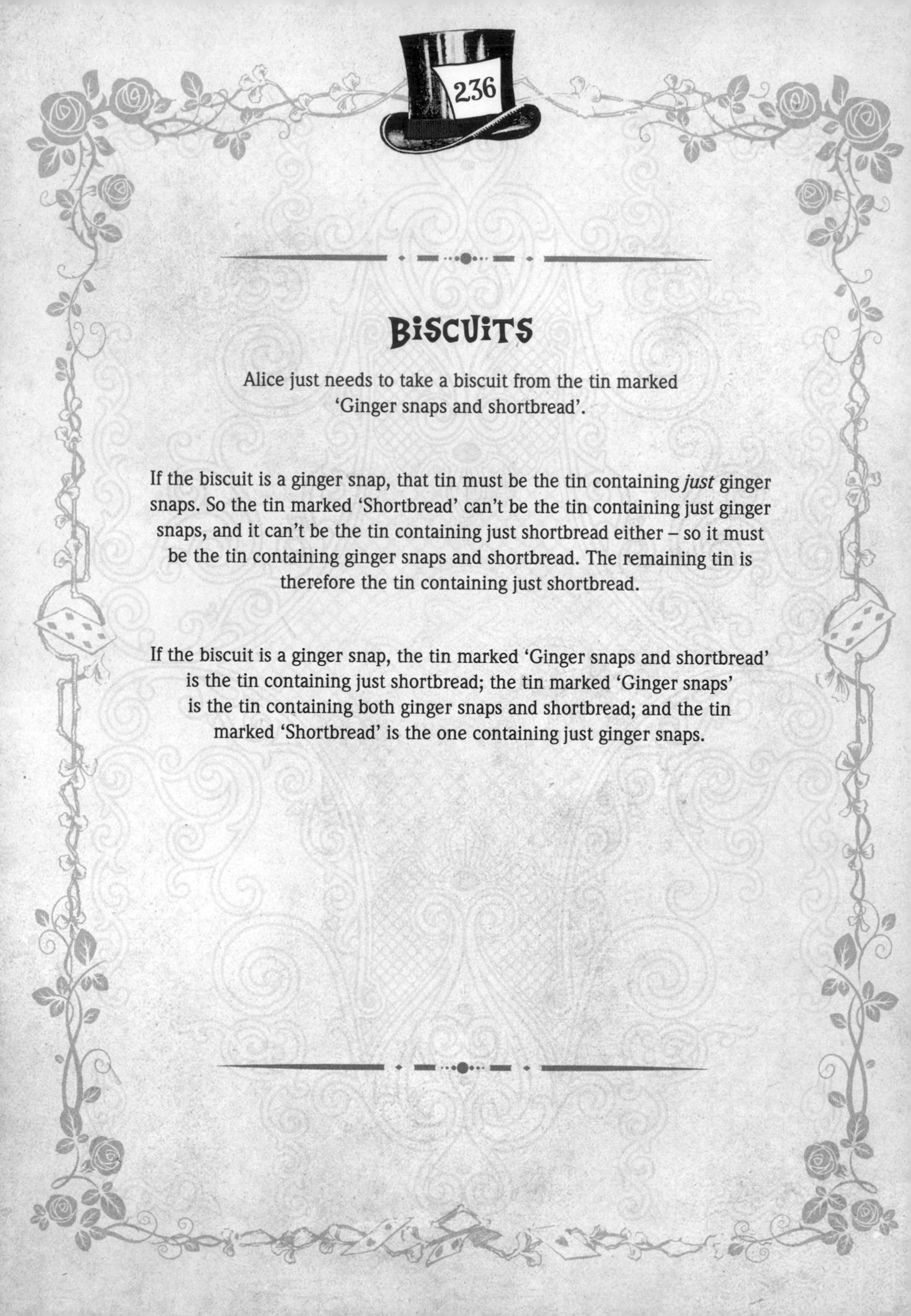

Biscuits

Alice just needs to take a biscuit from the tin marked 'Ginger snaps and shortbread'.

If the biscuit is a ginger snap, that tin must be the tin containing *just* ginger snaps. So the tin marked 'Shortbread' can't be the tin containing just ginger snaps, and it can't be the tin containing just shortbread either – so it must be the tin containing ginger snaps and shortbread. The remaining tin is therefore the tin containing just shortbread.

If the biscuit is a ginger snap, the tin marked 'Ginger snaps and shortbread' is the tin containing just shortbread; the tin marked 'Ginger snaps' is the tin containing both ginger snaps and shortbread; and the tin marked 'Shortbread' is the one containing just ginger snaps.

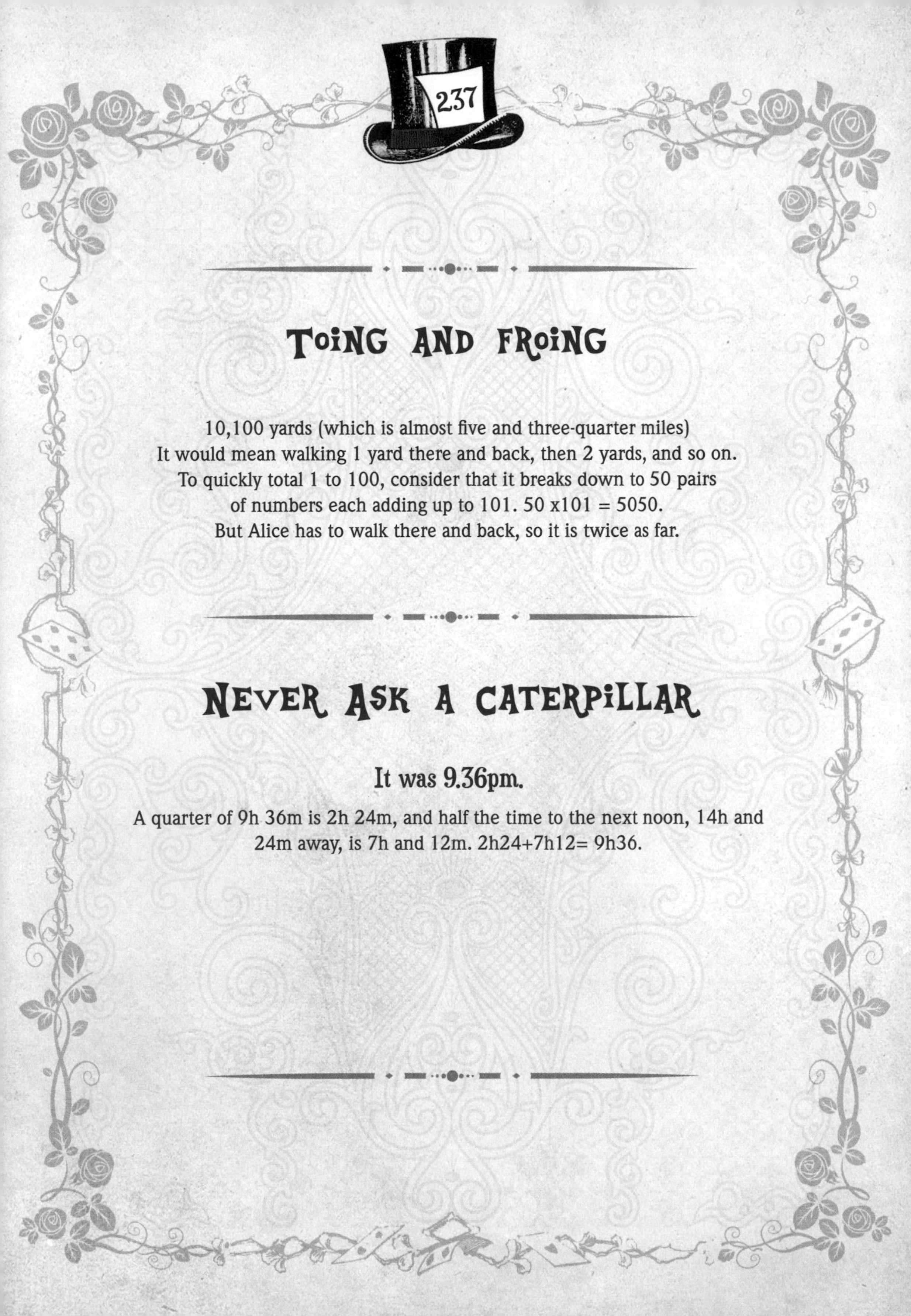

Toing and Froing

10,100 yards (which is almost five and three-quarter miles)
It would mean walking 1 yard there and back, then 2 yards, and so on.
To quickly total 1 to 100, consider that it breaks down to 50 pairs of numbers each adding up to 101. 50 x101 = 5050.
But Alice has to walk there and back, so it is twice as far.

Never Ask a Caterpillar

It was 9.36pm.

A quarter of 9h 36m is 2h 24m, and half the time to the next noon, 14h and 24m away, is 7h and 12m. 2h24+7h12= 9h36.

On Her Majesty's Service

Yes. If Fox was on duty, Fish could go off-duty.

A Wonderful Number

The number is 142857, 1/7th of 999999.
The six-digit length and the six multipliers (including x1) are indicators that it is derived from a fraction of 7.

THE QUEEN'S TREASURER

If speaking in terms of whole numbers, the treasurer's answer was correct. However, in financial terms a fourth is one-third as big as three-fourths, as illustrated below:

A SHORT SPRING

There must have been 1 (6 + 7 – 9) or 2 completely clear days, so there were 9 + 2 or 11 days in the period.

SPOT THE DIFFERENCE

FATHER WILLIAM'S SONS

15, 18 and 21. Two of the ages will always equal double the third. This can be expressed as $a + c = 2b$.

Now, going back to the instance when two of their ages equals the third, we can describe their ages as x, y, and $(x + y)$. At the same time, $a + c = 2b$ has to hold true. There's no way (after they're born) that $x + y = 2(x + y)$, so $x + (x + y)$ must $= 2y$ (we don't know which age x is, so it doesn't matter that we picked that instead of y). That means $2x + y = 2y$, or $y = 2x$ – so, in the first instance, we can write their ages as x, $2x$ and $(x+2x)$, or $3x$. The total of all those is $6x$, and we know that it has been ⅔ of that time since then, so it's been $4x$ more years. The ages of the sons are therefore now $5x$, $6x$ and $7x$, and that's an integer, because it's the 21st birthday of one of them. 21 is divisible by 7 and not 5 or 6, so the sons are now 15, 18 and 21. When they were 3, 6, and 9, which was 12 years ago, the two younger equalled the oldest; all through their lives, the oldest and youngest sons' ages will equal twice the middle son's.

INSTANT MESSAGING

The Frog Footman can be at any point between the Queen and the Duchess, facing either way. To prove this, at the end of one hour place the Footman anywhere between the Queen and the Duchess, facing in either direction. Reverse all the motions, and all three will return at the same instant to the starting point.

A NICE DAY FOR A WALK

6.25 minutes. The carriage they meets at 12.5 minutes has 2.5 minutes to reach its destination and start back, so is travelling 12.5/2.5 = 5 times faster than they are. Now, consider the total distance the Queen and Alice have to travel from when they initially start walking to when they are overtaken as x, and the distance the carriage has to travel in the same time as $x + y$, where y is the inbound 15-minute journey. Given the speed ratio, $x + y = 5 \times x$, or $y = 4x$, and $x = y/4$. We know that y takes 15 minutes, so x – the extra distance on top of a whole journey before the carriage overtakes them – takes 15/4, or 3.75 minutes.

Therefore both the carriage and the ladies have been travelling for a total 15 + 3.75 minutes = 18.75 minutes when the carriage overtakes them. It originally passed them after 12.5 minutes, so the extra time required is 18.75 – 12.5 = 6.25 minutes.

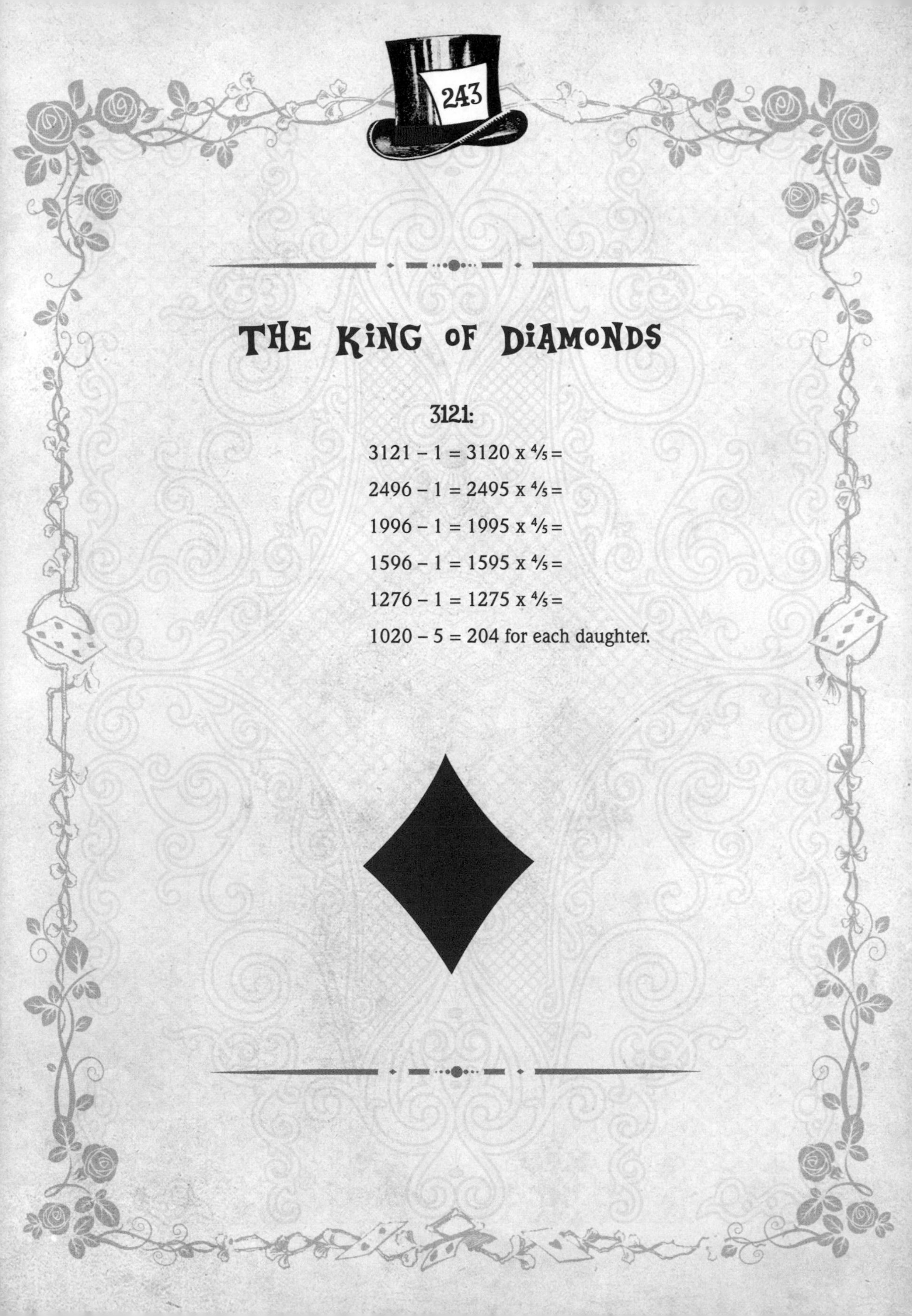

The King of Diamonds

3121:

3121 – 1 = 3120 x ⅘ =

2496 – 1 = 2495 x ⅘ =

1996 – 1 = 1995 x ⅘ =

1596 – 1 = 1595 x ⅘ =

1276 – 1 = 1275 x ⅘ =

1020 – 5 = 204 for each daughter.

SPOT THE DIFFERENCE

A GAME OF BRIDGE

The Queen dealt the bottom card to herself, then continued dealing from the bottom counter-clockwise.

YOU AREN'T OLD FATHER WILLIAM

44 years old.

His age + 6 years is equal to 5/4 of (age – 4), or 5x (age – 4) /4.

Multiply out by 4 to get rid of that divisor, and 4 x age + 24 = 5x (age - 4),

or 5 x age – 20. Add the 20 to both sides, and 4 x age + 44 = 5 x age or 44 years old.

THREE IS A CROWD

Alice shouldn't fire at anybody. By firing her first potato into the air she gives herself the best chance of all three. She should not shoot at the Red Knight because she if she hits him, White will eliminate her on the next shot. If Alice aims at and hits the White Knight, Red will have first shot against her and his overall probability of winning the duel will be 6 in 7, hers only 1 in 7. By deliberately missing, she will have the first shot against either White or Red on the next round. With a probability of 2 in 3, Red will hit White, and she will have an overall winning probability of 3 in 7, with a 1 in 3 probability that Red will miss White, in which case White will dispose of his stronger opponent (the Red Knight) and Alice's overall chance against White will be 1 in 3.

By shooting into the air, Alice's probability of winning the truel is 25 in 63 (about 40 per cent). Red's probability is 8 in 21 (about 38 per cent), and White's is only 2 in 9 (about 22 per cent).

To Catch a Dodo

First determine how far Alice would travel to catch the Dodo if the Dodo and Alice both ran forward in a straight line. Add to this the distance that Alice would travel to catch the Dodo if they ran toward each other on a straight line. Divide the result by 2 and you have the distance that Alice travels.

In this case, the Dodo is 250 yards away, and the speeds of Alice and the Dodo are in the proportion of 4 to 3. So, if both ran forward in a straight line, Alice would travel 1,000 yards to overtake the Dodo. If they travelled toward each other, Alice would travel $\frac{4}{7}$ of 250, or 142 and $\frac{6}{7}$ yards. Adding the two distances and dividing by 2 gives 571 and $\frac{3}{7}$ yards for the distance travelled by Alice. Since the Dodo runs at $\frac{3}{4}$ the speed of Alice, it will have travelled $\frac{3}{4}$ of Alice's distance, or 428 and $\frac{4}{7}$ yards.

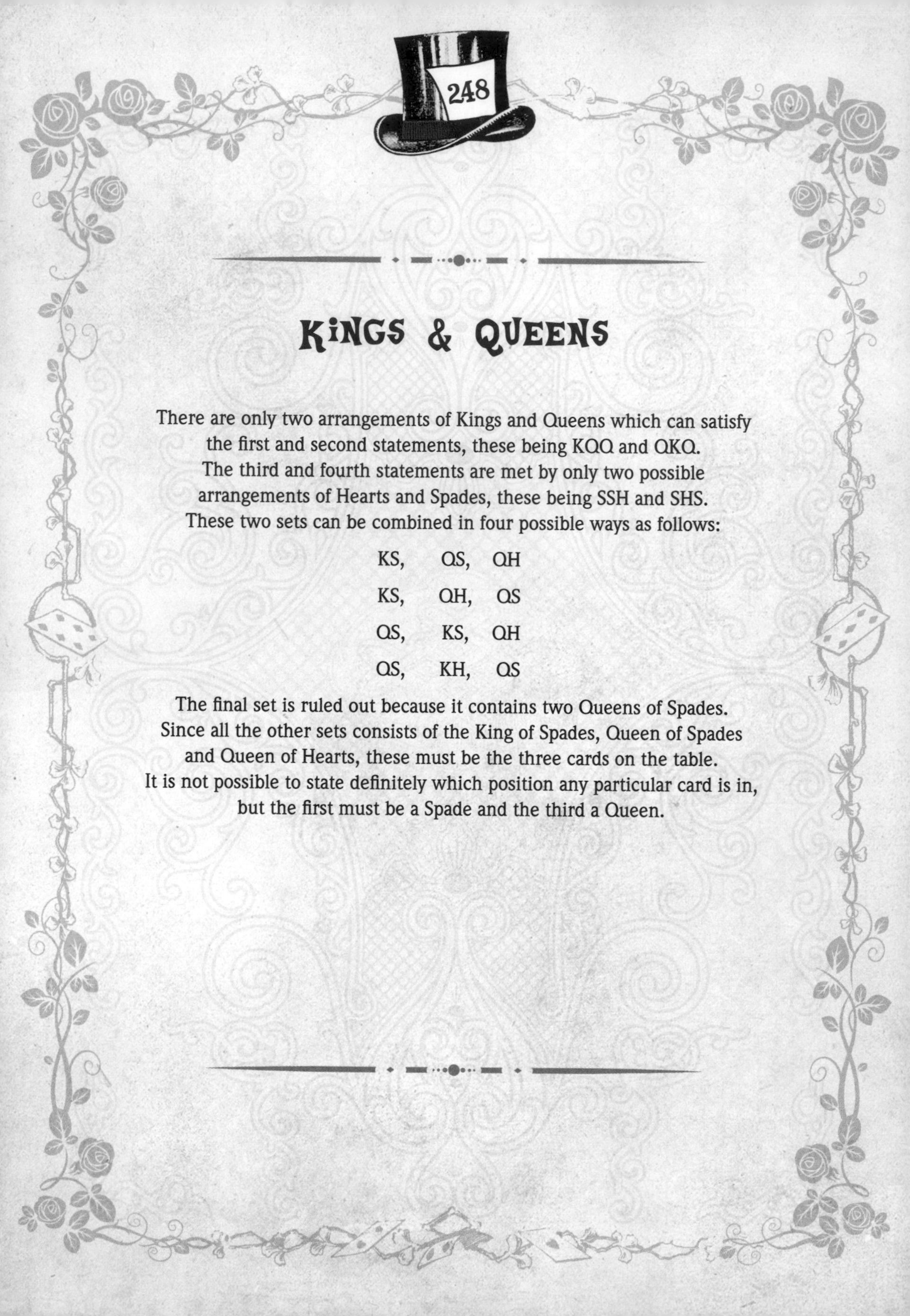

Kings & Queens

There are only two arrangements of Kings and Queens which can satisfy the first and second statements, these being KQQ and QKQ.
The third and fourth statements are met by only two possible arrangements of Hearts and Spades, these being SSH and SHS.
These two sets can be combined in four possible ways as follows:

KS, QS, QH

KS, QH, QS

QS, KS, QH

QS, KH, QS

The final set is ruled out because it contains two Queens of Spades.
Since all the other sets consists of the King of Spades, Queen of Spades and Queen of Hearts, these must be the three cards on the table.
It is not possible to state definitely which position any particular card is in, but the first must be a Spade and the third a Queen.

QUEENS' MOVE

If Alice is to win two games in a row, she must win the second game, so it is to her advantage to play that game against the weaker opponent. She must also win at least once against the stronger opponent, the White Queen, and her chances of doing so are greater if she plays the White Queen twice. The first game should therefore be against the White Queen.

A FAIR DEAL?

Yes, it is, because the probability that at least one card will be dealt as it is named is almost ⅔.

THE NORTH POLE

If West and East were stationary points, and West on your left when advancing towards North, then after passing the Pole and turning around, West would be on your right. But West and East are not fixed points, but *directions* round the globe. So wherever you stand facing North you will have the West direction on your left and the East on your right.

SWEET SISTERS

	Alice	Edith	Lorina
	4 sweets	3 sweets	14/3 sweets
or	12 sweets	9 sweets	14 sweets
Total	264	198	308
Ages	6	4½	7

THE QUEEN'S MARBLES

"Four marbles," said Alice without hesitation, "now, if you'll excuse us, we have a tea party to go to."

Only two marbles can be transferred out of the first bag. The contents of the two bags will then be one of the following:

	First Bag			Second Bag		
	Col A	Col B	Col C	Col A	Col B	Col C
1st possibility	3	3	1	3*	3*	5
2nd possibility	3	2	2	3	4	4

To assure at least 2 of each colour in the first bag, at least 7 marbles must be transferred back, because the first 6 might be the 3 Colour A and the 3 Colour B marbles represented by the starred 3s in the first possibility shown above. Therefore, there will be 4 marbles remaining in the second bag.

OYSTERS FOR SALE

We know each oyster was sold for the same number of pounds as there were oysters in the haul. If the number of oysters is n, the total number of pounds received was n^2. This was paid in £10 notes plus an excess of less than 10 pound coins. Since the Carpenter drew both the first and last notes, the total amount must contain an odd number of tens, and since the square of any multiple of 10 contains an even number of tens, n must end in a digit, the square of which contains an odd number of tens.
Only two digits, 4 and 6, have such squares: 16 and 36.
Both squares end in 6, so n^2 is a number ending in 6.
Thus the excess amount consisted of six pound coins.

After The Walrus took the £6, he still had £4 less than the Carpenter, so to even things up he wrote out a cheque for £2.

SPOT THE DIFFERENCE

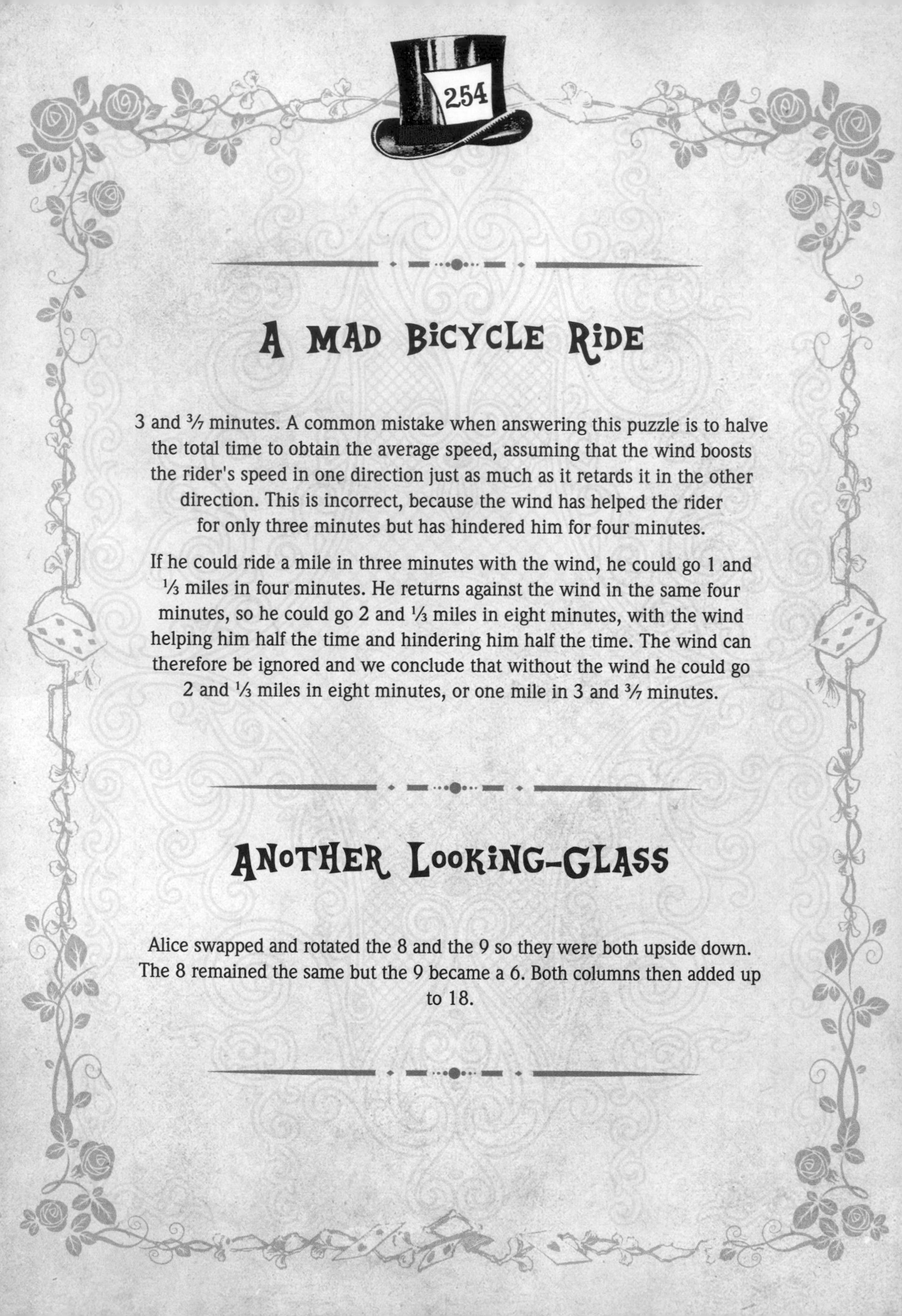

A Mad Bicycle Ride

3 and 3/7 minutes. A common mistake when answering this puzzle is to halve the total time to obtain the average speed, assuming that the wind boosts the rider's speed in one direction just as much as it retards it in the other direction. This is incorrect, because the wind has helped the rider for only three minutes but has hindered him for four minutes.

If he could ride a mile in three minutes with the wind, he could go 1 and 1/3 miles in four minutes. He returns against the wind in the same four minutes, so he could go 2 and 1/3 miles in eight minutes, with the wind helping him half the time and hindering him half the time. The wind can therefore be ignored and we conclude that without the wind he could go 2 and 1/3 miles in eight minutes, or one mile in 3 and 3/7 minutes.

Another Looking-Glass

Alice swapped and rotated the 8 and the 9 so they were both upside down. The 8 remained the same but the 9 became a 6. Both columns then added up to 18.

AFTERMATH

Five.

Total the number of injuries. That amount over 300 (which represents the hundred men who each have three injuries distributed amongst themselves) will be the minimum number of men who have all four.
64 + 62 + 92 + 87 = 305.

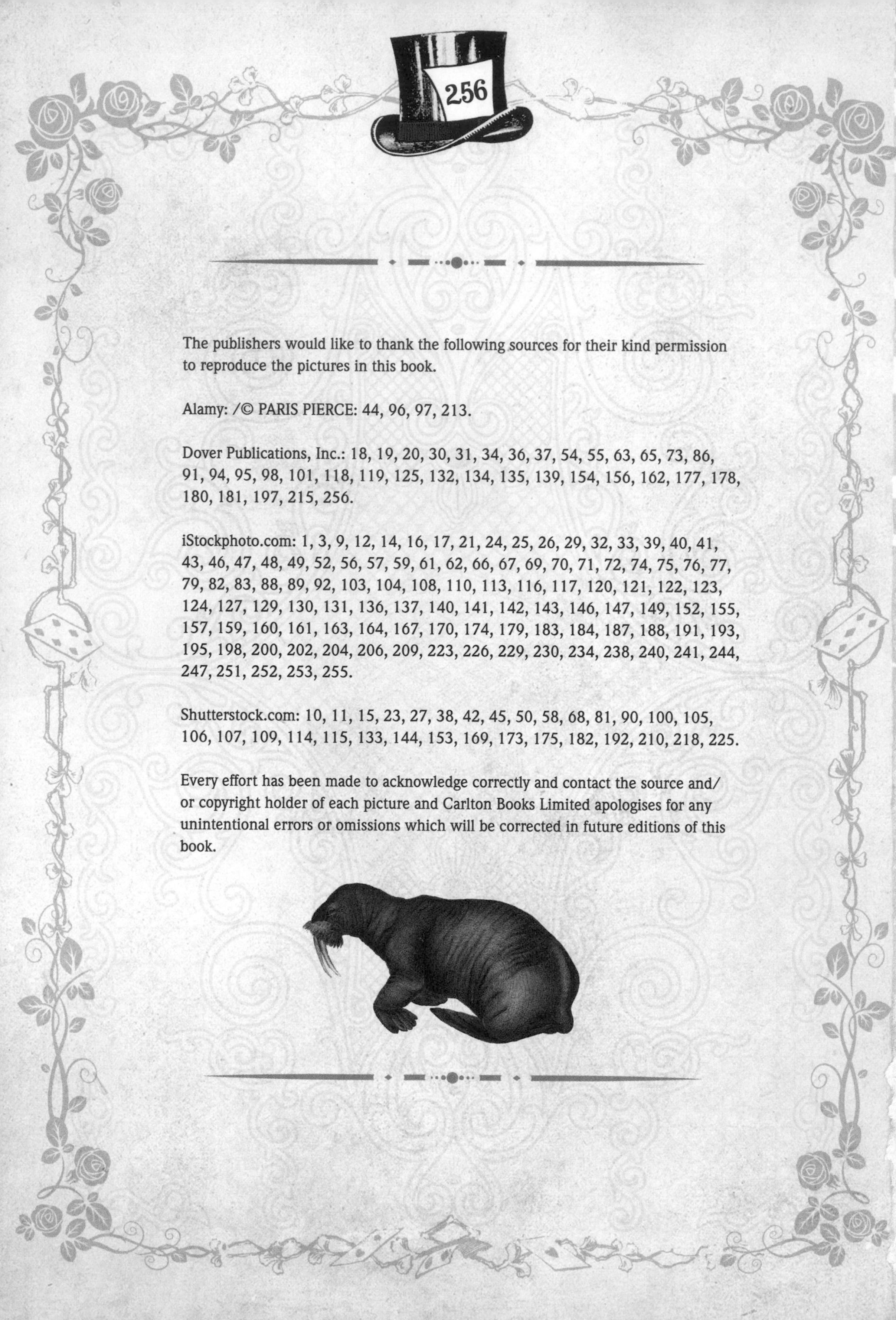

The publishers would like to thank the following sources for their kind permission to reproduce the pictures in this book.

Alamy: /© PARIS PIERCE: 44, 96, 97, 213.

Dover Publications, Inc.: 18, 19, 20, 30, 31, 34, 36, 37, 54, 55, 63, 65, 73, 86, 91, 94, 95, 98, 101, 118, 119, 125, 132, 134, 135, 139, 154, 156, 162, 177, 178, 180, 181, 197, 215, 256.

iStockphoto.com: 1, 3, 9, 12, 14, 16, 17, 21, 24, 25, 26, 29, 32, 33, 39, 40, 41, 43, 46, 47, 48, 49, 52, 56, 57, 59, 61, 62, 66, 67, 69, 70, 71, 72, 74, 75, 76, 77, 79, 82, 83, 88, 89, 92, 103, 104, 108, 110, 113, 116, 117, 120, 121, 122, 123, 124, 127, 129, 130, 131, 136, 137, 140, 141, 142, 143, 146, 147, 149, 152, 155, 157, 159, 160, 161, 163, 164, 167, 170, 174, 179, 183, 184, 187, 188, 191, 193, 195, 198, 200, 202, 204, 206, 209, 223, 226, 229, 230, 234, 238, 240, 241, 244, 247, 251, 252, 253, 255.

Shutterstock.com: 10, 11, 15, 23, 27, 38, 42, 45, 50, 58, 68, 81, 90, 100, 105, 106, 107, 109, 114, 115, 133, 144, 153, 169, 173, 175, 182, 192, 210, 218, 225.

Every effort has been made to acknowledge correctly and contact the source and/ or copyright holder of each picture and Carlton Books Limited apologises for any unintentional errors or omissions which will be corrected in future editions of this book.